CHOPIN

Books by David Whitwell

Philosophic Foundations of Education
Foundations of Music Education
Music Education of the Future
The Sousa Oral History Project
The Art of Musical Conducting
The Longy Club: 1900–1917
A Concise History of the Wind Band
Wagner on Bands
Berlioz on Bands
Aesthetics of Music in Ancient Civilizations
Aesthetics of Music in the Middle Ages
Aesthetics of Music in the Early Renaissance

The History and Literature of the Wind Band and Wind Ensemble Series

www.whitwellbooks.com

DAVID WHITWELL

CHOPIN: A SELF-PORTRAIT

WHITWELL BOOKS • AUSTIN, TEXAS, USA

Chopin: A Self Portrait
Second Edition
Dr. David Whitwell

WHITWELL PUBLISHING
815-A BRAZOS ST. #491
AUSTIN, TX 78701
WWW.WHITWELLPUBLISHING.COM

Composed in Bembo Book.
Published in the United States of America.
All images used in this book are in the public domain except where otherwise noted.

ISBN-13: 978-1-936512-40-9
ISBN-10: 1936512408

FOREWORD

This volume is not intended to be a traditional biography in which the reader is relegated to the position of being only an observer of the events of the subject's life as they parade before him on the pages of a book. The purpose of this volume is quite different for here we will pass by the daily events and happenings of Chopin's life and concentrate instead on his own thoughts, expressed in his own words.

The format has been to present Chopin's thoughts chronologically by subject in order to permit the reader not only an insight into his thinking on a particular subject, but the opportunity to study its development during his lifetime. The only references to individual compositions are those which offer the reader a unique view of how Chopin himself viewed the composition.

In the hope of allowing the reader the most intimate possible relationship with this master composer, I have resisted the strong and constant urge to add connecting or amplifying text and have instead left Chopin's own thoughts to speak for themselves. My own reading of this material has left me feeling a much closer relationship with Chopin the man than I have found in reading traditional biographies of him. It was this experience which impelled me to make this material available to others.

David Whitwell
Austin, Texas

ACKNOWLEDGEMENT

We wish to acknowledge our gratitude to the graphic artist, Daniel Ferla, for his important help in making possible this new edition of a work first published in 1986.

FRÉDÉRIC CHOPIN

Born March 1, 1810, Chopin was a true prodigy, exploring poetry, Polish folk music and composing several outstanding compositions all by the age of sixteen.

Formal musical studies began in 1826 at the Warsaw Conservatory, under Elsner, followed by his formal entry into the professional musical scene with a successful recital in Vienna at age nineteen.

Following two years of travel and composition, Chopin arrived in Paris in September 1831, where he was rapidly accepted into the highest musical and social circles and, in turn, through his sympathies with the city and its people it became his most permanent home. Professionally his time was taken primarily by teaching and composing; his extraordinary reputation as a pianist being based on only the rarest public appearances (perhaps no more than thirty in his lifetime!).

In 1836 Chopin began his ten-year relationship with Aurore Dudevant, the novelist known as George Sand. His life with her and her two children offered not only a period of domestic life, but a period of tranquility for composition and maternal care for the tuberculosis which was beginning to take its toll.

Chopin's illness, together with the domestic changes as Sand's children reached maturity, caused an eventual separation, which marked the beginning of the final stage of his life. The 1848 Revolution, together with its consequent impact on the musical life of Paris, contributed to Chopin's willingness to accept invitations to travel to England and Scotland. The state of both his physical and mental health, not to mention the language and cultural barriers, made this entire experience painfully difficult for the composer. When he returned to die in Paris the following year, he was not yet forty years of age.

Table of Contents

Part III: Chopin's Reflections on his own Music

Appendices

Three Remarkable First Person Descriptions of Chopin

Part I

Chopin: A Self-Portrait

Chapter One

Chopin on his Personality and Character Traits

1818

I could express my feelings more easily if they could be put into notes of music.[1]

1. Letter to his Father, December 6, 1818.

1823

Don't show this letter to anyone, because everyone would say that I can't write and don't know anything about politics.[2]

2. Letter to Eustachy Marylski, Warsaw, September, 1823.

1824

You are not the only one who rides, for I can stick on too. Don't ask how well, but I can ride enough for the horse to go slowly whenever he prefers, while I sit fearfully on his back, like a monkey on a bear.[3]

3. Letter to Wilhem Kolberg, Szafarnia, August 19, 1824.

1825

I'm as inquisitive about everything as an old woman.[4]

4. Letter to his Parents, Kowaloso, 1825.

I have had some very good times...gossiping, joking, singing, crying, laughing, fisticuffing, and so on.[5]

5. Letter to Jan Bialoblocki, Warsaw, July 8, 1825.

1828

I have seen Spontini, Zelter and Mendelssohn, but did not speak with any of them as I felt shy about introducing myself.[6]

6. Letter to his Family, Berlin, September 20, 1828.

1829

I am well and happy. I don't know why, but I appear to astonish the Germans, and I am astonished at their finding anything to be astonished at.[7]

7. Letter to his Family, Vienna, August 8, 1829.

You know how lazy I am ... [8]

8. Letter to Tytus Wojciechowski, Warsaw, October 3, 1829.

1830

Sennewald asked for my portrait, but I could not allow that, as it would be too much at once. I don't want anyone to wrap up butter in me, as happened with Lelewel's portrait.[9]

9.   Letter to Tytus Wojciechowski, Warsaw, March 27, 1830.

The Official Bulletin declared that the Poles should be as proud of me as the Germans are of Mozart — obvious nonsense.[10]

10. Letter to Tytus Wojciechowski, Warsaw, April 10, 1830.

Today I saw Soliwa … He is affectionate to my face, but it's worthless. I am polite but don't go near him when I can possibly help it …
How often I take night for day, and day for night. How often I live in my dreams and sleep in the daytime.[11]

11. Letter to Tytus Wojciechowski, Warsaw, April 17, 1830

You doubtless observe my tendency to do wrong against my will. As something has involuntarily crept into my head through my eyes, I love to indulge it, even though it may be all wrong.[12]

12. Letter to Tytus Wojciechowski, Warsaw, May 15, 1830.

If you suspect any love affair, as many persons in Warsaw do, forget it and believe that where my ego is concerned I can rise above all that. If I were in love I would manage to conceal the impotent and miserable passion for another few years. I sing my own praises the way dealers do with their wares.

If only my health lasts, I hope to work all my life. Something I wonder whether I really am lazy, whether I ought to work more when my physical strength allows it. Joking apart, I have convinced myself that I really am not such a hopeless vagabond, and that when necessity compels me I can do twice as much work as I do now.

You are not the master of your thoughts, but I am and I won't be thrown over any more than trees will give up foliage that brings them life and joy and character. Even in winter it shall be green in my heart.[13]

13. Letter to Tytus Wojciechowski, Warsaw, September 18, 1830.

I am often quite absent-minded. If I have something before my eyes that interests me, horses could trample over me and I should not see them …

There's one thing in which I don't imitate you, that is in taking sudden decisions.[14]

14. Letter to Tytus Wojciechowski, Warsaw, September 22, 1830.

Yesterday morning Hummel came to me with his son, who is finishing my portrait. It is so like me that it could not be better. I am sitting on a stool, in a dressing gown, with an inspired expression of I don't know what.[15]

15. Letter to his Family, Vienna, December, 1830.

People say I have grown fat.[16]

16. Letter to his Family, Vienna, December 1, 1830.

1831

As an artist I am still in the cradle, but as a Pole I have begun my third decade.[17]

17. Letter to Joseph Elsner, Vienna, January 26, 1831.

I lack nothing except more life and spirit. I am tired, but sometimes as cheerful as at home. Then again there are days when you can't get two words out of me and no understanding why.

I have let my mustache grow on the right side, and it is quite long. There is no need for it on the left side because it is the right side that faces the public.[18]

18. Letter to his Family, Vienna, July, 1831.

You know how easily I make acquaintances and how I like to gossip with people.[19]

19. Letter to Tytus Wojciechowski, Paris, December 25, 1831.

1832

Though this is only my first year among the artists here, I have their friendship and respect. I am ashamed of all this bosh that I have written; I have been boasting like a child. I would scratch it out, but have no time to write another sheet. Anyhow, perhaps you have not forgotten what my character is like. If so, you will remember that I am today what I was yesterday.

Myself I am a revolutionist. I care nothing for money, only for friendship.[20]

20. Letter to Dominik Dziewanowski, Paris, 1832.

1833

You know me well enough to know that unfortunately I never do what I ought to do.[21]

21. Letter to Auguste Franchomme, Paris, September, 1833.

1838

Imagine me, without white gloves or hair curling, as pale as ever, in a cell with such doors as Paris never had for gates.[22]

1839

It is not my fault that I am like that fungus which looks like a mushroom, but poisons those who pull it up and taste it, mistaking it for something else. I know that I have never been of any use to anyone — but also not very much to myself.[23]

I am not fitted to give concerts, the public frightens me, I feel suffocated by its panting breath, paralyzed by its curious glance, mute before those unknown faces.[24]

1845

I was not made for the country, though fresh air is good for me. I don't play much, as my piano is out of tune.

I feel strange here this year. Often in the morning I go into the next room, but there is no one there. At this moment I am not with myself, but only as usual in some strange outer space. Granted, it is only those imaginary spaces, but I am not ashamed of that.[25]

Oh, how time goes! I don't know how it is, but I can't do anything of any value and yet I am not idle. I don't wander from corner to corner, as I did with you. I just sit whole days and evenings in my room.[26]

1848

Misfortune and misfortune. I have lost all desire in my soul.[27]

What I have left is just a big nose and an undeveloped fourth finger.[28]

If I were younger, perhaps I would go in for a mechanical life, give concerts all over the place and succeed in a not unpleasant career (anything for money!). But now it is hard to start turning oneself into a machine.[29]

22. Letter to Juljan Fontana, Palma, December 28, 1838.

23. Letter to Juljan Fontana, Marseilles, March 7, 1839.

24. Quoted by Liszt, in Frederic Chopin. Translated by Edward N. Waters. London: Collier-Macmillan, 1963, 84.

25. Letter to his Family, Nohant, July 20, 1845.

26. Letter to his Family, Nohant, October 1, 1845.

27. Letter to Wojciech Grzymala, London, May 13, 1848.

28. Letter to Juljan Fontana, Edinburgh, August 18, 1848.

29. Letter to his Family, August 19, 1848.

I want to do the best, and I am sure I shall do the worst. But that is my fate. No one can escape his destiny.[30]

30. Letter to Mlle de Rozieres, Keir, October 20, 1848.

Friendship is all very well, but gives no right to anything further. I have made that clear. Even if I could fall in love with someone, as I should be glad to do, still I would not marry, for we should have nothing to eat and nowhere to live. And a rich woman expects a rich man, or if a poor man at least not a sickly one, but one who is young and handsome. It is bad enough to go to pieces alone, but two together, that is the greatest misfortune. I may die in a hospital, but I won't leave a starving wife behind me.[31]

31. Letter to Wojciech Grzymala, London, November, 1848.

CHAPTER TWO

Chopin on his Physical and Mental Health

1825

My health is as good as a faithful dog.[32]

32. Letter to his Parents, Kowalowo, 1825.

1826

Everyone is falling ill, and I too. You maybe suppose that all this scribbling is being done at a table, but you are wrong. It is from under my quilt and comes out of a head that is tied up in a nightcap because it's been aching, I don't know why, for the last four days. They have put leeches on my throat because the glands have swelled and our Roemer says it is a catarrhal affection.[33]

33. Letter to Jan Bialoblocki, Warsaw, February 12, 1826.

If this letter seems to you rather wild, don't be surprised because I am not well.[34]

34. Letter to Jan Bialoblocki, Warsaw, June, 1826.

The fresh air and the whey which I take very conscientiously have set me up so well that I am quite different from what I was in Warsaw ... but one thing is lacking, for which not all the beauties of Reinertz can compensate me: a good instrument. Imagine, Sir, that there is not one good piano. All that I have seen are instruments which cause me more distress than pleasure.[35]

35. Letter to Jozef Elsner, Reinertz, August, 1826.

I have been drinking whey and the local waters for two weeks and they say that I am looking a little better, but I am said to be getting fat.

Near Reinertz there is a mountain with rocks known as Heu-Scheuer, from which there is a wonderful view. But the air at the very top is not good for everyone and, unluckily, I am one of those patients to whom it is not allowed.[36]

36. Letter to Wilhelm Kolberg, Reinertz, August 18, 1826.

Both German and German-Polish doctors have told me to walk as much as possible. I go to bed at nine. All teas, evenings and balls are off. I drink an emetic water by Malcz's orders and feed myself only on oatmeal like a horse.[37]

37. Letter to Jan Bialoblocki, Warsaw, November 2, 1826.

1828

I have managed to acquire much energy in the licensed Prussian diligences. They certainly seem to have agreed with me, for I am well, and very well.[38]

38. Letter to his Family, Berlin, September 16, 1828.

1829

You wouldn't believe how dreary I find Warsaw now. If it weren't for the family making it a little more cheerful, I should not stay. But how dismal it is to have no one to go to in the morning to share one's griefs and joys; how hateful when something weighs on you and there's nowhere to lay it down. I often tell to my piano what I want to tell to you.[39]

39. Letter to Tytus Wojciechowski, Warsaw, October 3, 1829.

You can't think how much I feel something is missing in Warsaw now. I have no one I can speak two words to, no one to turn to with confidence.[40]

40. Letter to Tytus Wojciechowski, Warsaw, November 14, 1829.

1830

Today I was more bored than ever. I wish I could throw off the thoughts that poison my happiness, and yet I love to indulge in them. I don't know myself what is wrong with me.

How often I take night for day, and day for night, how often I live in my dreams, and sleep in the daytime — worse than sleep, because I feel just the same and instead of recuperating during that state of numbness, as one does in sleep, I get weaker and more tired than ever.[41]

41. Letter to Tytus Wojciechowski, Warsaw, April 17, 1830.

Christmas Day. Today I am sitting alone, in a dressing-gown, gnawing my ring and writing.[42]

42. Letter to Jan Matuszynski, Vienna, December 25, 1830.

1831

It is not amusements that are lacking, but the desire for them, and I have not gone in for them in Vienna as yet. Today is New Year's – how sadly I begin it! Perhaps I shall not end it.[43]

43. Letter to his Family, Vienna, January 1, 1831.

As I write this, some horrible presentiment torments me. I keep thinking that it's a dream or hallucination, that I am with all of you and all this is a dream. The voices I hear, to which my soul is not accustomed, make no other impression on me than the rattling of carriages in the street or any other casual noise. Your voice or that of Tytus would rouse me from this dead state of indifference. To live or to die seems all one to me today.[44]

44. Letter to Jan Matuszynski, Vienna, Spring, 1831.

Today it was beautiful on the Prater. Crowds of people with whom I have nothing to do. I admired the foliage, the spring smell and that innocence of nature brought back my childhood's feelings.

A storm was threatening so I went in, but there was no storm. Only I got melancholy. Why? I don't care for even music today. It is late, but I am not sleepy; I don't know what is wrong with me. And I've started my third decade!

The papers and posters have announced my concert. It is to be in two day's time and it's as if there were no such thing; it doesn't seem to concern me. I don't listen to compliments; they seem to me stupider and stupider. I wish I were dead, and yet I should like to see my parents Everything I have seen abroad till now seems to me old and hateful, and just makes me sigh for home, for those blessed moments that I didn't know how to value. What used to seem great today seems common. What I used to think common is now incomparable, too great, too high. The people here are not my people. They are kind, but kind from habit. They do everything too respectably, flatly, moderately. I don't want even to think of moderation. I'm puzzled, I'm melancholy and I don't know what to do with myself. I wish I weren't alone![45]

45. Chopin's Diary, Vienna, Spring, 1831.

I am quite well, and enjoying myself finely.[46]

46. Letter to his Family, Vienna, May 28, 1831.

I lack nothing except more life and spirit; I'm tired, but sometimes as cheerful as at home. When I get a melancholy mood, I go to Pani Szaszek; there I usually find several nice Polish women whose sincere and really hopeful talk always gives me so good an opinion of myself f that I begin to imitate the Viennese generals … Then again there are days when you can't get two words out of me and no understanding why.[47]

I go nearly crazy with melancholy, especially if it rains.[48]

My health is bad. I am gay on the outside, especially among my own folk (I count Poles as my own); but inside something gnaws at me — some presentiment, anxiety, dreams, or sleeplessness, melancholy, indifference, desire for life and in the next instant desire for death. Some kind of sweet peace, some kind of numbness, absent-mindedness; and sometimes definite memories worry me. My mind is sour, bitter, salt, some hideous jumble of feelings shakes me![49]

1833
People say I have gown fatter and look well, and I feel splendid.[50]

1835
Forgive me that I can't collect my thoughts and write about anything else but that we are happy at this minute, that I had only hope and now have the realization, and am happy, happy, happy.[51]

1837
Last winter I was ill again with grippe and was sent to Ems.[52]

I am really not well.[53]

The doctor orders me to Ems.[54]

1838
I am in Palma. A glorious life! I am better.[55]

I have been as sick as a dog these last two weeks. I caught cold in spite of the heat, roses, oranges, palms, figs and three most famous doctors on the island. One sniffed at what I spat up, the second tapped where I spat it from, the third pokes about and listened how I spat it. One said I had died, the second that I am dying and the third that I shall die. And today I'm the same as ever, only I can't forgive Jasio for not giving me a consultation when I had an attack of bronchite aigue,

47. Letter to his Family, Vienna, July, 1831.

48. Letter to Tytus Wojciechowski, Paris, December 12, 1831.

49. Letter to Tytus Wojciechowski, Paris, December 25, 1831.

50. Letter to Auguste Franchomme, Paris, September, 1833.

51. Letter to his Family, Carlsbad, August 16, 1835.

52. Letter to Anton Wodzinski, Paris, May or June, 1837.

53. Letter to Wojciech Grzymala, Paris, undated.

54. Letter to Teresa Wodzinska, Paris, June 18, 1837.

55. Letter to Juljan Fontana, Palma, November 19, 1838.

which can always be expected in my case. I could scarcely keep them from bleeding me, and they put no setons or vesicators; but thanks to Providence I am now as before.[56]

56. Letter to Juljan Fontana, Palma, December 3, 1838.

I can't sleep, only cough and, covered with poultices for a long time past, wait for the spring or for something else.[57]

57. Letter to Juljan Fontana, Palma, December 14, 1838.

1839

Thanks for the friendly help that you give to a feeble person. Embrace Jas; tell him that I am — or rather, that they were not allowed to bleed me, that I have vesicators, that I don't cough much, only in the morning and that I am not yet regarded at all as a consumptive. I drink no coffee, nor wine — only milk. I keep warm and look like a girl.[58]

58. Letter to Juljan Fontana, Marseilles, March 7, 1839.

I am better with every day … although the doctor will not let me leave the south till the summer.[59]

59. Letter to Juljan Fontana, Marseilles, March 13, 1839.

I am still weak and not fit to write.[60]

60. Letter to Juljan Fontana, Marseilles, March 17, 1839.

My health is quite restored.[61]

61. Letter to Ernest Canut, Marseilles, March 28, 1939.

Sometimes I play for myself, but have not yet begun to sing and dance.[62]

62. Letter to Juljan Fontana, Marseilles, April 25, 1939.

I am not well, and [George Sand] is ailing … [a postscript by George Sand expresses concern that Chopin is becoming 'devoured by melancholy.'][63]

63. Letter to Wojciech Grzymala, Nohant, July 8, 1839.

We are as happy as children.[64]

64. Letter to Wojciech Grzymala, Nohant, [undated] 1839.

1840

I cough and do nothing.[65]

65. Letter to Juljan Fontana, Paris, April 23, 1840.

1842

I must stay in bed all day, I have so much pain in my beastly face and glands.[66]

66. Letter to Wojciech Grzymala, [Paris] March?, 1842.

1843

I believe that we are both well, that illness is far from me and that I have only happiness before me.[67]

67. Letter to George Sand, Paris, September 26, 1843.

1844

I will say nothing more except that I am well and that I am your most fossilized fossil.[68]

68. Letter to George Sand, Paris, September 23, 1844.

1845

Today the entire household has colds. That I cough insufferably is not surprising.

Sometimes I would give years of my life for a few hours of sunshine. I have outlived so many persons younger and stronger than I, that I think I must be immortal.[69]

69. Letter to his Family, Paris, October 12, 1845.

I am as sick as a dog.[70]

70. Letter to Wojciech Grzymala, undated..

1847

Here there is nothing but illness on illness.[71]

71. Letter to George Sand, Paris, January 17, 1847.

This year my attacks … have not been frequent, in spite of the extreme cold …

My head is not always equally clear.[72]

72. Letter to his Family, Paris, April 19, 1847.

Princess Marcellina has come for a few weeks … I am too ill to find rooms for them.[73]

73. Letter to Wojciech Crzymala, Paris, September 17, 1847.

I choke; I have a headache.[74]

74. Letter to Solange Clesinger, Paris, November 24, 1847.

There is a great deal of grippe, but I have enough with my usual cough. I smell my homeopathic flasks from time to time, give many lessons in the house, and manage as I can.[75]

75. Letter to his Sister, Paris, December 25, 1847.

1848

I have been in bed for several days with a frightful grippe.[76]

76. Letter to Solange Clesinger, Paris, February 17, 1848.

I have had neuralgia all last week.[77]

77. Letter to Solange Clesinger, Paris, March 3, 1848.

This morning I am breathing a little better, but the whole of this last week I have not felt too well.[78]

78. Letter to Auguste Franchomme, London, May 1, 1848.

I am breathing better just these last days, because it is only these days that the sun has shown its face.[79]

79. Letter to Adolf Gutman, London, May 6, 1848.

If I could have a few days without blood-spitting, if I were younger, if I were not prostrate under my afflictions as I am, I might be able to start life again.[80]

80. Letter to Wojciech Grzymala, London, June 2, 1848.

I can't find any comfort, I have worn out all feeling — I only vegetate and wait for it to end soon.[81]

81. Letter to Wojciech Grzymala, London, July, 1848.

My health varies from hour to hour, but often in the mornings it seems as if I must cough my life out. I'm depressed in spirit, but my head gets muddled. I even avoid solitude, so as not to think for I must not be ill long here and want to avoid getting feverish …

I can't finish your letter; my nerves are all on the jump. I suffer from some kind of silly depression and with all my resignation — I don't know — I worry about what to do with myself.[82]

82. Letter to Wojciech Grzymala, London, July, 1848.

My health might be worse, but I am weaker all the time, and still unable to bear this climate.[83]

83. Letter to Auguste Franchomme, Edinburgh, August 6, 1848.

La table d'harmonie is excellent, but the strings have snapped and some of the pegs are missing. The worst is that we are the work of a fine instrument maker, some Stradivarious sui generic, who is no longer here to repair us …

I'm writing you rubbish because there's no sense in my head. I'm vegetating and waiting patiently for winter. I dream now of home, now of Rome, now of joy, now of grief. Nobody plays as I like nowadays and I have grown so forbearing that I could listen with pleasure to Sowinski's Oratorio and not die. I remember Norblin, the painter, saying that a certain painter in Rome had seen the work of another one and found it so unpleasant that he died. What I have left is just a big nose and an undeveloped fourth finger.[84]

84. Letter to Juljan Fontana, Edinburgh, August 18, 1848.

The climate does not agree with me very well. Yesterday and today I have been spitting blood, but, as you know, with me that does not mean much. I made the railway journey from London to Edinburgh by the Express train, 407 miles in 12 hours and it may have been a little too much for me.[85]

85. Letter to Wojciech Grzymala, August 19, 1848.

The weather has changed. It is bad outside and I am cross and depressed. People bore me with their excessive attentions. I can't breathe, I can't work. I feel alone, alone, alone, though I am surrounded.[86]

86. Letter to Wojciech Grzymala, September 4, 1848.

For me the future grows always worse. I am weaker, I can't compose anything, less from lack of desire than from physical hindrances.[87]

87. Letter to Wojciech Grzymala, Keir, October 1, 1848.

I have been ill the last eighteen days, ever since I reached London. I have not left the house at all. I have had such a cold and such headaches, short breath and all my bad symptoms.

Why should God kill me this way, not at once, but little by little and through the fever of indecision?[88]

88. Letter to Wojciech Grzymala, London, October 18, 1848.

I am progressively weaker, duller, without any hope, without a home.[89]

89. Letter to Wojciech Grzymala, Edinburgh, October 30, 1848.

What has become of my art? And my heart, where have I wasted it? I scarcely remember anymore, how they sing at home. That world slips away from me somehow, I forget. I have no more strength. If I rise a little, I fall again, lower than ever.[90]

90. Letter to Wojciech Grzymala, London, November, 1848.

1849

I have to lie down ten times a day. Molin knew the secret of how to liven me up. Since then I have seen M. Louis; Dr. Roth, during two months, and now M. Simon, who has a great reputation among the homeopaths, but they just sound me and give no relief. They all agree about climate, peaceful life, rest. Rest — I shall get it one day without them.[91]

91. Letter to Solange Clesinger, Paris, January, 30, 1849.

For the moment, everything is disgusting.[92]

92. Letter to Solange Clesinger, Paris, April 13, 1849.

I am stronger, for I have been eating and have dropped the medication, but I gasp and cough just the same only I bear it better …

I can't find out from my Dr. Frenkel, whether to go to some watering-place, or to go south. He has again withdrawn his infusion and given me another medication and again I don't want it. When I ask him about hygiene, he answers that a regular regime is not necessary for me … He may be a very good consultant … but he has no sequence in his mind.[93]

My Jew, Dr. Frenkel, has not come for a week. At the end he even left off putting papers into the urine, only talked to me about some Englishman whom he saved from cholera by means of some medicine which the reactionary French government will not have him asked to introduce. So I am left to myself and perhaps may crawl out all the quicker.[94]

His Esculapius has not called for ten days. He has probably guessed, at last, that there is something beyond his science here. All the same, praise him up well to your lodger and to others who know him and say that he did me a lot of good, but that I am the sort of person who is satisfied the moment he gets a little better.[95]

I have not spat blood since the day before yesterday, my legs are swollen but I'm still weak and lazy. I can't go upstairs, I suffocate.[96]

A recent blood-splitting changes my traveling plans for the moment.[97]

I am very weak. I have some sort of diarrhea. Yesterday I consulted Cruveille, who advises me to take almost nothing and just keep still. He said that if homeopathy had done me good in Molin's time, that was because it did not overload me with medications and left much to nature. But I see that he also regards me a consumptive, for he ordered a teaspoonful of something with lichen in it.[98]

The doctors do not allow me to travel at all. I drink Pyrenean waters in my room.[99]

As this cough will choke me, I implore you to have my body opened, so that I may not be buried alive.[100]

93. Letter to Wojciech Grzymala, Paris, June 18, 1849

94. Letter to Wojciech Grazymala, Chaillot, June 22, 1849.

95. Letter to Ludwika Jedrzejewicz, Paris, June 25, 1849.

96. Letter to Wojciech Grzymala, Paris, July 2, 1949.

97. Letter to Solange Clesinger, Paris, July 4, 1849.

98. Letter to Wojciech Grzymala, Paris, July 10, 1849.

99. Letter to Tytus Wojciechowski, Paris, August 20, 1849.

100. Final request of Chopin, written shortly before his death.

CHAPTER THREE

Chopin on his Daily Life

1826

It is true that from Saturday to Thursday I was out every evening until two in the night. But that is not why I am ill, because I always slept it off in the morning.[101]

When you learn about my life style you will agree that it is difficult to find a moment for sitting at home. In the morning, at six o'clock at the latest, all the patients are at the wells. Then there is an atrocious band of wind players, a dozen caricatures of various types collected together, the head one a thin bassoonist with a stuffy, spectacled nose. They frighten all the ladies that are afraid of horses by playing to the freely perambulating Kur-Gäste. Then there is a sort of rout, or rather a masquerade, not everyone in masks for those are only a small proportion, besides those who 'get hanged for company.' This promenade, along the beautiful avenues that connect the Establishment with the town, usually lasts until eight, or according to the number of glasses that people have to drink in the morning. Then everyone goes home for breakfast. After breakfast people usually go for a walk. I walk until twelve and then one has to eat dinner, because after dinner one has to go back to Brunn. After dinner there is usually a bigger masquerade than in the morning because everyone is dressed up, all in different clothes from those of the morning. Again there is vile music and it goes until evening. As I have to drink only two glasses of Lau-Brunn after dinner I get home to supper fairly early. After supper I go to bed.[102]

1828

There's a room upstairs which is to be at my service and steps have been made to it from the wardrobe room. I am to have an old piano there, and an old bureau, and it's to be my den.[103]

101.   Letter to Jan Bialoblocki, Warsaw, February 12, 1826.

102.   Letter to Wilhelm Kolberg, Reinertz, August 18, 1826.

103.   Letter to Tytus Wojciechowski, Warsaw, December 27, 1828.

1830

Your advice about evening parties is sound and I have declined several invitations to them.[104]

104.   Letter to Tytus Wojciechowski, Warsaw, April 10, 1830.

Yesterday at Bayer's we danced the mazurka. Slawik lay on the floor to represent a sheep and some old German Contessa with a big nose and a pockmarked face did some kind of queer waltz step with long thin legs, holding her skirts gracefully with two fingertips in the ancient manner.[105]

105.   Letter to his Family, Vienna, December, 1830.

Let me describe to you my life here. I am on the 4th floor. It is true it is in the best street, but I should have to look well out of the window to see what is gong on there. My room is big and comfortable, with three windows, the bed opposite the windows, a splendid piano [pantaloon] on the right side, a sofa on the left, mirrors between the windows, in the middle a fine, big rounded mahogany table and a polished parquet floor.

It is quiet after dinner, His Lordship does not receive guests, so I can concentrate my thoughts on all of you. In the morning I am called by an insufferably stupid servant. I get up, they bring me coffee, I play and mostly have a cold breakfast. About nine comes the maître for the German language; after that I usually play. Then Hummel [the composer's son] has been drawing me, and Nidecki learning my concerto. All this in a dressing-gown until noon.

After noon comes a very worthy German, Leidenfrost, a German who works at the prison, and if the weather is fine we go for a walk on the glacis around the town. After this I go to dinner, if I am invited anywhere. If not, we go together to the place frequented by the entire academic youth, that is the Zur Boemische Köchin. After dinner black coffee is drunk in the best Kaffeehaus. That is the custom here. Then I pay visits, return home at dusk, curl my hair, change my shoes and go out for the evening. About ten, eleven or sometimes midnight, never later, I come back, play, sleep, read, look, laugh, go to bed, put the light out and always dream about some of you.[106]

106.   Letter to Jan Matuszynski, Vienna, December 25, 1830.

1831

Today I got up early and practiced until two, then I went
out to dine.[107]

Mechetti arranged a surprise, a concert for Malfatti, Wild,
Cicimara, Fräulein Emmerling, Fräulein Lutzer and my
noble self performed some important music. I never heard
the quartet from Moses better sung. Wild was in good voice
and I acted as conductor. Cicimara said that no one in Vienna
accompanies so well as I (and I thought, 'I know that as
well as you.' Hush!) A huge crowd of strangers listened to
the music from the terrace. The moon shone superbly, the
fountains played, a delicious smell from the orangey they have
put up filled the air, in a word, a glorious night and a most
gorgeous place.

You can't imagine how beautifully designed is the salon in
which they sang: huge windows thrown wide, from which
you can see all Vienna, plenty of mirrors and very few lights.
The extra length of the adjoining oblong vestibule on the
left gave an enormous spaciousness to the whole room. The
genuine amiability of our host, the elegance and comfort, the
merry company, the witty conversation that was the order
of the day and the excellent supper kept us sitting late. It was
about midnight when we got into the carriages and dispersed
for home …

A few days ago I spent the evening at Fuchs'. He showed
me his collection of 400 autograph scores, among which is
my Rondo for two pianos, bound. Fuchs gave me a sheet of
Beethoven's handwriting.[108]

I am at Boulevard Poissonière, Nr. 27. You would not
believe what a delightful lodging it is. I have a little room
beautifully furnished with a mahogany table and a balcony
over the boulevard from which I can see from Mont Martre to
the Pantheon and the whole length of the fashionable quarter.
Many persons envy me my view, but none my stairs.[109]

I can't refrain from telling you my adventure with Pixis.
Imagine, he has a very pretty fifteen year old girl living with

107.   Letter to his Family, Vienna,
May 28, 1831.

108.   Letter to his Family, Vienna,
June 25, 1831.

109.   Letter to K. Kumelski, Paris,
September 18, 1831.

him, whom it is said he thinks of marrying and whom I met
when I visited him in Stuttgart. Pixis, on arriving here, invited
me to call but did not mention that the girl, whom I had
forgotten, had arrived with him. (I might have called sooner,
had I known). He asked to call on him, so after a week I went.
On the stairs I was pleased to see the young pupil and she asked
me in, saying that Herr Pixis was out but it did not matter.
Come in and rest and he will soon be back, etc. We both feel a
little tremulous. Knowing that the old man is jealous, I excuse
myself. I will come again, and so on. Meanwhile, as we stand
discussing prettily on the stairs in the innocence of our hearts,
up comes the little Pixis. He looks through large spectacles to
see who is on the stairs and talking to his belle. Hurrying up the
stairs the poor fellow stops in front of me and says brusquely,
'Bon jour,' and to her, 'Q'est'ce que vous faites ici?' and a huge
jeremiad of German devils at her for daring to receive young
men during his absence. I also, smiling and ignoring everything,
upheld Pixis, scolding her for going out so lightly clad, and so
on. At last the old man realized, swallowed, took me by he arm,
conducted me into the salon and didn't know where to put me
to sit, he was so afraid I should take offense and play some trick
on him in his absence, or else murder the pupil. (I could not hide
my amusement at the joke of anybody supposing me capable of
that sort of thing). How do you like it? I, as seducteur![110]

110. Letter to Tytus Wojciechowski, Paris, December 12, 1831.

1838

I am in Palma, among palm trees, cedars, cacti, olives,
pomegranates, etc. Everything the Jardin des Plantes has in
its greenhouses. A sky like turquoise, a sea like lapis lazuli,
mountains like emerald, air like heaven. Sun all day and hot;
everyone in summer clothing; at night guitars and singing for
hours. Huge balconies with grape-vines overhead; Moorish
walls. Everything looks toward Africa, as the town does. In
short, a glorious life!

Go to Pleyel; the piano has not yet come. I shall probably
lodge in a wonderful monastery, the most beautiful situation
in the world: sea, mountains, palms, a cemetery, a crusaders'
church, ruined mosques, aged trees, thousand-year-old olive
trees. Ah, my dear, I am coming alive a little. I am near to what
is most beautiful. I am better.[111]

111. Letter to Juljan Fontana, Palma, November 19, 1838.

Nature is benevolent here, but the people are thieves because they never see strangers and so don't know how much to demand. Oranges can be had for nothing, but a trouser button costs a fabulous sum. But all that is just a grain of sand when one has this sky, this poetry that everything breathes here, this coloring of the most exquisite places, color not yet faded by men's eyes. No one has yet scared away the eagles that soar every day above our heads![112]

112. Letter to Juljan Fontana, Palma, December 28, 1838.

1839

My door is shut to all musical and literary amateurs.[113]

113. Letter to Juljan Fontana, Marseilles, March/April, 1839.

Marseilles is ugly. An old, but not ancient place; it bores us.[114]

114. Letter to Wojciech Grztmala, Marseilles, March 27, 1839.

In 5, 6 or 7 days I shall be in Paris. I forgot to ask you to order a hat for me from my Dupont in your street. He has my measure and knows how light I need them. Let him give me this year's fashion, not exaggerated; I don't know how you dress now. Also go in, as you pass, to Dautremont, my tailor on the boulevard and tell him to make me a pair of grey trousers at once. You can choose the shade of dark grey; winter trousers, good quality, without belt, smooth and stretchy. You're an Englishman, you know what I want. Also a plain black velvet waistcoat, but with a tiny inconspicuous pattern, something very quiet and elegant.[115]

115. Letter to Juljan Fontana, Nohant, October 3, 1839.

The apartment sounds splendid, only why is it so cheap? Isn't there some very unpleasant 'but'? Is it all right, does it smell bad, or is it dirty, or are there so many neighbors that you can't go to the privy alone? Is there a cornet à piston in the house or some such thing?[116]

116. Letter to Juljan Fontana, Nohant, October 4, 1839.

1841

A few days ago I received your pianoforte, for which I thank you most warmly. The instrument arrived in good tune, almost in chamber-concert tune. But I have not yet played on it much, as the weather is so fine that I am out of doors nearly all the time.[117]

117. Letter to Camille Pleyel, [August, 1841]

Don't tell Pleyel he has sent me a very bad pianoforte.[118]

118. Letter to Juljan Fontana, August 16, 1841.

Please send me a description of the apartment on the first floor, with the number and details: are there stairs? Does one have to enter near the street? Is it high? Does it smoke? Is it dark? I should like to be somewhere in the Montblanc or Marthurins, or on the boulevard near the Chaussee d'Antin.[119]

119. Letter to Juljan Fontana, Nohant, September 13, 1841.

1845

I am sorry you cannot be with us and Delacroix this evening at the Conservatoire, to hear Haydn's Creation. It is only the second concert we are attending this year; the first was the day before yesterday, with Mozart's Requiem.[120]

120. Letter to Stefan Witwicki, Paris, Easter, 1845.

I have moved my piano. It is by the wall where the little sofa and table used to be. The bureau at which I write stands in the middle; on the left lie some of my music papers, in front of the repeater you sent me, in its case, with roses and pinks, pens and a bit of sealing-wax.[121]

121. Letter to his Family, Nohant, July 20, 1845.

1846

Mr. Faber, a professor of mathematics in London, has exhibited a very ingenious automaton which he calls Euphonia. It pronounces fairly clearly not one or two words, but long sentences and still more surprising sings an aria of Haydn and 'God save the Queen.' If the directors of opera could have many such androids they could do without chorus singers, who cost a lot and give a lot of trouble. It's a strange thing, to get to that by means of levers, bellows, valves, little chains, pipes, springs, etc. I once wrote to you about Vaucanson's drake, which digested what it age. Vaucanson also made an android that played on the flute. But until now no machine has sung, 'God save the Queen,' with the words.[122]

122. Letter to his Family, Nohant, October 11, 1846.

1847

Yesterday I sat down at a table after dinner to look at the album of a certain painter who has traveled about America for 16 years. I could not put it down (Wonderful things!). But too many to see at one time.[123]

123. Letter to his family, Paris, April 19, 1847.

1848

Erard was very courteous and placed a piano at my disposal. I have one instrument of Broadwood and one of Pleyel, three in all. But what is the use, when I have not the time to play on them. I have innumerable visits to pay and my days flash past like lightning.[124]

124. Letter to Adolf Gutman, London, May 6, 1848.

It is not even laziness that has kept you from hearing anything from me, but just time thrown away on nothing. I can't get out of bed before eight. My Italian, who is concerned with himself and his accounts, wastes my time in the morning. After ten begin tribulations which bring in no money and, about one, a few lessons. I can neither walk nor be very active, so I can't get about over my affairs, but I see that they are going somehow.[125]

125. Letter to Wojciech Grzymala, London, May 13, 1848.

Yesterday I was at dinner with J. Lind, who afterwards sang me Swedish things until midnight. They are as distinctive in character as our Polish things. We have something Slavonic, they something Scandinavian, which are totally different, and yet we are nearer to each other than the Italian to the Spaniard.[126]

126. Letter to Wojciech Grzymala, London, May 13, 1848.

Those with whom I was in the closest harmony have also died for me, even Ennike, our best tuner, has drowned himself. So now I have not left in the world even a piano tuned as I am used to having it. Moos has died and nobody makes such comfortable shoes for me now. If another four or five desert me for St. Peter's gates, all the comforts of my life will be gone ad patres.[127]

127. Letter to Juljan Fontana, Edinburgh, August 18, 1848.

Among the notabilities is Lady Byron, with whom I am on very friendly terms. We converse, like the goose with the sucking pig, She in English, I in French. I understand why she bored Byron.[128]

128. Letter to his Family, August 19, 1848.

I have had a queer adventure, which luckily ended in nothing but might have cost my life. We were driving in the neighborhood, above the sea. The carriage we were in was a coupe, with two very fine young thoroughbred English horses. One horse began to prance, caught its leg and started to kick. The other horse did the same thing and as they bolted on a slope in the park, the reins dragged, the coachman fell from his box and was badly knocked about. The carriage was smashed with banging from tree to tree. We were just tumbling over the precipice when a tree stopped the carriage. One horse broke loose and bolted frantically; the other fell under the carriage. The windows were broken by branches. Luckily nothing happened to me except a few bruises on my legs from the jolting. The footman jumped out cleverly, so only the carriage was smashed and the horses injured. The person who saw it from the distance screamed that two persons were killed, as they saw one flung out and the other falling on the ground. Before the horse moved, I was able to get out of the carriage and am all right. No one who saw it, and no one of us who were there, can understand how we were not smashed to pulp. I was reminded of the Berlin ambassador in the Pyrenees, who was dashed about that way. I confess to you that I contemplated my last hour with composure, but the thought of broken arms and legs disconcerted me. To be crippled would be the last straw.[129]

129.   Letter to Wojciech Grzymala, September 4, 1848.

The whole morning, until two o'clock, I am fit for nothing now, and then when I dress everything strains me and I gasp that way until dinner time. Afterwards one has to sit two hours at the table with the men, look at them talking and listen to them drinking. I am bored to death, I am thinking of one thing and they of another, in spite of all their courtesy and French remarks at the table. Then I go to the drawing-room where it takes all my efforts to be a little animated, because then they usually want to hear me. And then my good Daniel carries me up to my bedroom (as you know that is usually upstairs here), undresses me, gets me to bed, leaves the light on, and I am free to breathe and dream until it is time to go somewhere else, for my Scottish ladies give me no peace.[130]

130.   Letter to Wojciech Grzymala, Keir, October 1, 1848.

Apart from all else, my kind Scottish ladies are boring me again. Mrs. Erskine, who is a very religious Protestant, good soul, would perhaps like to make Protestant of me. She brings me the bible, talks about the soul, quotes the psalms to me. She is religious, poor thing, but she is greatly concerned about my soul. She is always telling me that the other world is better than this one and I know all that by heart and answer with quotations from Scripture and explain that I understand and know about it.[131]

131. Letter to Wojciech Grzymala, London, October 18, 1848.

My Scotswomen are kind. I have not seen them for two or three weeks but they are coming today. They want me to stay and go on dragging me around the Scottish palaces, here and there and everywhere, as I am invited. They are kind, but so boring that the Lord preserve them!

Every day I get letters, and answer none of them and wherever I go, they come after me.[132]

132.   Letter to Wojciech Grzymala, London, November, 1848.

I do not go out, except sometimes to the Bois de Boulogne. The Scottish ladies have just come. They stifle me with boredom.[133]

133.   Letter to Wojciech Grzymala, Paris, June 18, 1848.

CHAPTER FOUR

Insights into Chopin's General Outlook on Life

1830

How dismal it must be to die anywhere else except where one has lived! How horrible it will be to see beside my deathbed some cold-blooded doctor or servant instead of my own family.

Explain to me why man supposes that today is only going to be tomorrow …

A man can't always be happy. Perhaps joy comes for only a few moments in life, so why tear oneself away from illusions that can't last long anyhow …

It would be better if human beings knew neither money, nor porridge, nor boots, nor hats, nor beefsteaks, nor pancakes, etc.[134]

It's not as we would, but as we can.
I do think of my own good, and dedicate to it everything that I do for people. That is, for people to see, so that reputation, which means so much here, may not be unfavorable to me, it's only superficial, nothing inside.
Often trying to make oneself out better only makes one out worse.[135]

To say goodbye, that's the worst.[136]

1831

The day before yesterday … we went to St. Veit. It's a pretty place, but I can't say the same about the so-called Tivoli, where there is a sort of carrousel, or sliding on vehicles, what

134.   Letter to Tytus Wojciechowski, Warsaw, September 4, 1830.

135.   Letter to Tytus Wojciechowski, Warsaw, September 18, 1830.

136.   Letter to Tytus Wojciechowski, Warsaw, October 5, 1830.

they call a 'Rutsch.' It's an idiotic thing. However, crowds of people slide down in these things, for no object; I didn't even want to look at them. But afterwards, as there were eight of us, and all good friends, we began racing down to see who could go fastest, helping ourselves with our feet, competing with each other. And from being heartily disgusted with this silly Viennese game, I became an enthusiastic proselyte, until I recovered my senses and realized that these things are occupying strong and healthy bodies and muddling capable minds and this at a moment when humanity is calling on such to defend it. The devil take them![137]

137.   Letter to his Family, Vienna, July, 1831.

Moscow rules the world! Oh God, do You exist? You are there and You don't avenge it. How many more Russian crimes do You want — or are You a Russian too!!?[138]

138.   Chopin's Diary, Stuttgart, September, 1831.

Perhaps one frets more when things are easy.[139]

139.   Letter to Tytus Wojciechowski, Paris, December 12, 1831.

1838
Nature is a beautiful thing, but it's better to have no dealings with human beings.[140]

140.   Letter to Juljan Fontana, Palma, December 28, 1838.

1839
All will pass, and our tongues will rot, and our souls be unhurt.[141]

141.   Letter to Juljan Fontana, Nohant, August, 1839.

You know how easily things grow out of nothing, when they pass through a mouth that smears them all over and makes something else out of them.[142]

142.   Letter to Juljan Fontana, undated.

1845
Mr. Brunel ... has now invented ... a new locomotive, by means of which it will be possible to go 50 English miles an hour. That excessive speed will not make railway traveling pleasing.[143]

143.   Letter to his Family, Nohant, October 1, 1845.

The better health people usually have, the less patience they have in bodily suffering. There is no remedy for that in the world. Even the intellect is no help.[144]

144.   Letter to his Family, Nohant, October 12, 1845.

1847

I had forgotten that there are still so many persons with us who live without knowing how, why or to what end.[145]

145. Letter to his Family, Paris, April 19, 1847.

I have faith in things coming right little by little.[146]

146. Letter to Solange Clesinger, Paris, December 31, 1847.

1849

I am becoming stupider than ever, and I attribute it to the cacao which I take every morning instead of my coffee. Don't ever take cacao and prevent your friends from taking it.[147]

147. Letter to Solange Clesinger, Paris, January 30, 1849.

One can't have everything in this world. Be content with the greatest of joys: health.[148]

148. Letter to Solange Clesinger, Paris, April 5, 1849.

Luck is never the same in this world … I have no conversation left any more, except axioms of this kind, so forgive me if I tell them to you. Thus, for instance, I hope that the spring sunshine will be my best doctor.[149]

149. Letter to Solange Clesinger, Paris, April 13, 1849.

Youth is an obligation, that is to say you have an absolute duty to be happy.[150]

150. Letter to Solange Clesinger, Paris, May, 1849.

Wives ought always to obey their husbands.
Perhaps God will allow things to come right; and if God doesn't then at least act as if He would allow it. I have good hope of it for I seldom demand much …[151]

151. Letter to Ludwika Jedrzejewicz, Paris, June 25, 1849.

CHAPTER FIVE

Chopin on Women

1830

If you suspect any love affair, as many persons in Warsaw do, forget it and believe that, where my ego is concerned, I can rise above all that. If I were in love, I would manage to conceal the impotent and miserable passion for another few years.[152]

152. Letter to Tytus Wojciechowski, Warsaw, September 18, 1830.

On Sunday, being struck by an unexpected glance in church, I blundered out in a state of delightful torpor, and for a quarter of an hour didn't know what I was doing. Meeting Dr. Parys, I didn't know how to explain my confusion and had to make up a tale of a dog running under my feet and getting trodden on.[153]

153. Letter to Tytus Wojciechowski, Warsaw, September 22, 1830.

My turn for holidays will come one day. There are plenty of pretty German girls — but when will it come, when![154]

154. Letter to his Family, Vienna, December 1, 1830.

1831

In my mind I can see Konstancja Gladkowska before my eyes. I think I don't love her any more and yet I can't get her out of my head.[155]

155. Chopin's Diary, Vienna, Spring, 1831.

What a lot of charitable ladies! They just run after people …[156]

156. Letter to K. Kumelski, Paris, September 18, 1831.

1841

Mlle de Rozières an insufferable pig who has dug her way in some queer fashion into my private garden and is rooting about for truffles among the roses. She is a person to keep away from.[157]

157. Letter to Juljan Fontana, Nohant, August 25, 1841.

CHAPTER SIX

Chopin on his Professional Experiences

Chopin on his Career

1830

I am gradually launching myself in the world, but I have only one ducat in my pocket!

I expect to stay here three years.[158]

I already have a huge reputation among the artists here in Paris.[159]

1832

I have arrived in the highest society. I sit with ambassadors, princes, ministers and don't even know how it came about, because I did not try for it. It is a most necessary thing for me because good taste is supposed to depend on it. At once you have a bigger talent if you have been heard at the English or Austrian embassy. You play better if Princess Vaudemont was your protector.

Though this is only my first year among the artists here I have their friendship and respect. One proof of respect is that even people with huge reputations dedicate their compositions to me before I do so to them. Pixis has inscribed to me his last Variations with a military band, also people compose variations on my themes. Kalkbrenner has used my Mazurka, Op. 7, Nr. 1, in this way. The pupils of the Conservatoire, Moschele's pupils, those of Herz and Kalkrenner — in a word, finished artists, take lessons from me and couple my name with that of Field. In short, if I were still stupider than I am, I should think myself at the top of my career. Yet know how much I still lack to reach perfection. I see it the more clearly

158. Letter to K. Kumelski, Paris, September 18, 1831.

159. Letter to Tytus Wojciechowski, Paris, December 12, 1831.

now that I live only among first-rank artists and know what
each one of them lacks.[160]

1848

I have to go into society every evening till late. I am not
strong enough for such a life. If it only brought in money, but
until now I have had only two paid evenings at 20 guineas.
I give a few lessons in the house at a guinea and still have no
notion of a decent concert.

I have played before the Queen, and the Prussian Prince
Albert, and Wellington and all the most elegant persons, and at
the Duchess of Sutherland's. Everything apparently went very
well, but up to the 23rd the Court is in mourning for some
aunt, so nothing is going on and I doubt that I shall be invited
there. I don't want to play at the Philharmonic for it will
not give me a penny, only enormous fatigue: one rehearsal,
and that in public, and to have any success you must play
Mendelssohn. The great world usually gives only balls or vocal
concerts ...

I am introduced and don't know to whom and am not living
in London at all. Twenty years in Poland, seventeen in Paris —
no wonder I'm not brilliant here, especially as I don't know
the language. The don't talk when I play and they speak well
of my music everywhere. But they consider me some sort of
amateur and that I shall soon be a grand seigneur, because I
wear clean shoes and don't carry visiting cards stating that I
give lessons, play at evening parties, etc. Old Lady Rothschild
asked me how much I charge, because some lady who had
heard me had asked her about it. As Lady Sutherland had given
me 20 guineas, because Broadwood, on whose piano I play,
had suggested that price, I answered, 20 guineas. The good
lady, obviously kind, thereupon told me that it is true I play
very well, but that she advises me to take less, as moderation is
necessary this season.[161]

Next week I go to Scotland to a certain Lord Torphiken and
to Lady Murray. I will not enumerate a crowd of other oral
invitations, with their addresses, for I cannot drag from place
to place. That kind of life has disgusted me and I see no end to
it before me.[162]

160.   Letter to Dominik
Dziewanowski, Paris, undated
[1832].

161.   Letter to Wojciech Grzymala,
London, June 2, 1848.

162.   Letter to Wojciech Grzymala,
London, July, 1848.

After deducting lodging and carriage, all I shall have been able to scrape together will perhaps not come to more than 200 guineas ... In Italy you can live a year on that, but here, not half a year.

Perhaps the Queen's director has dug a pit for me because I did not return his call or because I would not play at the Philharmonic. If the season here lasted six months I could gradually get known after my fashion, but as it is, there is no time. Everything here is in such a rush.[163]

163. Letter to Wojciech Grzymala, London, July, 1848.

I have given two musical matinees, which people apparently enjoyed, but this does not prevent my having been equally bored. But without them I don't know how I could have managed the three months in expensive London, keeping up a large apartment, as I was forced to do there, a carriage and a manservant ...

What to do with myself next, I don't know. But I do earnestly wish that somebody would give me to the end of my life an annual pension for not composing, for never having invented a tune.

I shall follow only the advice of ... whoever advises me last, for I see it makes no practical difference how long I think about it.[164]

164. Letter to Auguste Franchomme, Edinburgh, August 6, 1848.

The Philharmonic Society invited me to play for them: a great favor, or rather honor. Everyone who comes here tries for it and this year neither Kalkbrenner nor Halle were invited in spite of much effort. Bit I refused and this produced a bad impression among musicians and especially among conductors. I refused once because I was not well, that was the reason I gave, but the real one was that I should only have had to play one of my concerti with the orchestra and these gentlemen give only one rehearsal, and that in public, with entrance by free tickets. How can you rehearse, and repeat! So we should have played badly ...[165]

165. Letter to his family, August 19, 1848.

Chopin on his Experiences as a Piano Soloist

1828

You know how nice it is, when you're sleepy and they ask you to improvise. Try to please everybody![166]

166. Letter to Tytus Wojciechowski, Warsaw, December 27, 1828.

1829

You know from my last letter, dearest Parents, that I have been persuaded to give a concert. So, yesterday, Tuesday evening at 7:00 in the Imperial and Royal Opera House I made my entry into the world! As I got nothing for it, and didn't try to get anything, Count Gallenberg organized the program as follows:

Beethoven, Overture to Prometheus
My Variations on 'La Ci Darem La Mano'
Singing by Miss Veltheim
My Rondo, Op. 5

Then more singing, then a short ballet.

At rehearsal the orchestra accompanied so badly that I substituted the Freie Phantasie for the Rondo. As soon as I appeared on the stage, the bravos began. After each variation the applause was so loud that I couldn't hear the orchestra's tutti. When I finished they clapped so much that I had to come out and bow a second time. The Freie Phantasie didn't go off quite so well, but there was a lot of clapping and bravos and I had to come out again. That was easier to do, because the Germans appreciate that sort of thing. You need have no anxiety for me and my reputation.

The stage manager of the theater was very kind and amiable to me. He was so encouraging with his assurances before I went on to the stage and kept my thoughts off it so well that I was not very nervous, especially as the hall was not full. At his request that I should also improvise on a Polish theme, I chose 'Chmiel,' which electrified the public, as they are not used to such songs. My spies in the stalls assure me that people even jumped on the seats.

All the same it is being said everywhere that I played too softly, or rather, too delicately for people used to the piano pounding of the artists here. I expect to find this reproach in the paper, especially as the editor's daughter thumps frightfully. It doesn't matter, there has always got to be a but somewhere and I should rather it were that one than have people say I played too loud.

Thus, my first appearance has been as fortunate as it was unexpected. Hube says that no one ever attains anything by ordinary methods and according to any prearranged plan, that one must leave something to luck. And it was just trusting to luck that I let myself be persuaded to give the concert. I decided that if the papers should so smash me that I could not again appear before the world I would take to interior house painting; it's easy to smear a brush across paper and one is still a son of Apollo.

Today I am wiser and more experienced by about four years.[167]

167.   Letter to his Family, Vienna, August 12, 1829.

The Schwarzenbergs, the Wobrzes, etc., all speak in high terms of the delicacy and elegance of my playing. Czerny has paid me a lot of compliments.[168]

168.   Letter to his Family, August 13, 1829

If I was well received the first time, it was still better yesterday. The moment I appeared on the stage there were bravos, repeated three times, and there was a larger audience. I have captured both the learned and the emotional folk. They will have something to talk about.[169]

169.   Letter to his Family, Vienna, August 19, 829

The orchestra was sulky at the rehearsal, chiefly, I think, because I had just arrived from nowhere and was already playing my own compositions. So I began the rehearsal with the Variations dedicated to you, which were to have been preceded by the Karakowiak Rondo. They went well, but I began the Rondo several times and the orchestra muddled it frightfully and complained of the bad manuscript. All the confusion was caused by pauses written differently at the top and bottom of the score, although I explained that only the top numbers count. It was partly my own fault, but I had thought they would understand. But they were annoyed at the inaccuracy and besides they are all virtuosi and composers too.

Anyhow they played so many tricks that I was just ready to fall ill for the evening. But Baron Demmar, the stage manager, seeing that it was a little lack of goodwill on the part of the orchestra, and because Würfel wanted to conduct and they won't like him, proposed that instead of playing the Rondo I should improvise. At that suggestion the orchestra opened big eyes. I was so annoyed that in desperation I consented. Maybe the risk and my bad temper were just the goad that stirred me up to do my best in the evening. I sat down, pale, with a rouged-up partner to turn the pages and who boasted to me that he had turned the pages for Moscheles, Hummel, Herz, etc. It was a magnificent instrument made by Graff, perhaps the finest one n Vienna. You may believe me that I played from desperation. The Variations produced such an effect that, apart from the clapping after each one, I was obliged to come back to the stage after finishing.

At the second concert Lichnowski, Beethoven's protector, wanted to give me his pianoforte for the concert, which was a great deal to offer. He thought mine was too weak in tone, but that is my way of playing, which, again, delights the ladies.[170]

1830

Regarding the first concert, the hall was full, with both the boxes and stalls sold out three days beforehand, but it did not produce in the mass of the audience the impression I expected. The first Allegro is accessible only to the few. There were some bravos, but I think only because they were puzzled — What is this? — and had to pose as connoisseurs! The Adagio and Rondo had more effect (one heard some spontaneous shouts), but as for the Potpourri on Polish Themes in my opinion it failed to come off. They applauded in the spirit of 'Let him go away knowing we were not bored.'

The Polish Courier ended by counseling 'more energy!' I guessed where this energy lies, so at the next concert I played on a Viennese piano instead of my own and consequently the audience, an even larger one than before, was pleased.

170. Letter to Tytus Wojciechowski, Warsaw, September 12, 1829.

Clapping, exclamations that I had played better the second time than the first, that every note was like a pearl, and so on … I improvised, which greatly pleased the first tier boxes. If I am to tell you the truth, I did not improvise as I should have wished to do, rather it was for the public.[171]

Yesterday's concert was a success. I was not a bit, not a bit nervous and played the way I play when I'm alone, and it went well. The final Mazurka elicited big applause, after which — the usual farce — I was called up. No one hissed and I had to bow four times — but properly now, because Brandt has taught me how to do it.

I don't know how things would have gone yesterday if Soliwa had not taken my scores home with him, read them and conducted so that I could not rush as if I would break my neck. But he managed so well to hold us all back, I assure you, I never succeeded in playing so comfortably with the orchestra.[172]

At the rehearsal the Germans admired my playing — 'how light his playing is!' — but said nothing about the compositions. Tytus even heard one person say, 'He can play, but not compose.'[173]

1831

When I was introduced to Kalkbrenner, he asked me to play something. I should have liked to hear him first, but, knowing how Herz plays, I put my pride in my pocket and sat down. I played my E minor, which the Rhinelanders, the Lindpainters, Bergs, Stuntzes, Schunks and all of Bavaria had so raved over. I astonished Kalkbrenner, who at once asked me, was I was not a pupil of Field, because I have Cramer's method and Field's touch. This delighted me.

He has convinced me that I can play admirably when I am in the mood and badly when I am not, a thing which never happens to him. After close examination he told me that I have no school, that I am on an excellent road but can slip off the tracks. He said that after his death, or when he finally stops playing, there will be no representative of the great pianoforte

171.   Letter to Tytus Wojciechowski, Warsaw, March 27, 1830.

172.   Letter to Tytus Wojciechowski, Warsaw, October 12, 1830.

173.   Letter to his Family, Breslau, November 9, 1830.

school. He said that even if I wish it, I cannot built up a new school without knowing the old one. In a word, that I am not a perfected machine and that his hampers the flow of my thoughts. He said I have a mark in composition and that it would be a pity not to become what I have the promise of being, and so on and so on.

Pleyel's pianos are non plus ultra.[174]

I am not fitted to give concerts, the public frightens me, I feel suffocated by its panting breath, paralyzed by its curious glance, mute before those unknown faces.[175]

1848

Pleyel, Perthuis, Leo and Albrecht have persuaded me to give a concert. All places have been sold out for a week. I shall give it in the Pleyel salon on the 16th of this month. Only 300 tickets, at 20 fr. I shall have the fashionable world of Paris. The King has taken 10, the queen 10, the Duchess of Orleans 10, the Duke of Montpensier 10, though the court is in mourning and none of them will come. They want to attend a second concert, which I probably will not give for even this one bores me.[176]

My friends came one morning and told me that I must give a concert, that I need not worry about anything and only sit down and play. All the tickets have been sold out for a week and all are at 20fr. The public is putting down names for a second concert, of which I am not thinking. The court has ordered 40 tickets and though the newspapers have merely said that perhaps I will give a concert, people have written to my publisher from Brest and from Nantes to reserve places. I am astonished at such eagerness and today I must play, if only for conscience's sake, for I believe I am playing worse now than ever before. I shall play, for the interest of it, Mozart's Trio with Franchomme and Alard. There will be no posters and no free tickets. The hall is conveniently arranged and has room for 300. Pleyel always jokes about my stupidity and will decorate the steps with flowers to make me more willing to play.[177]

174. Letter to Tytus Wojciechowski, Paris, December 12, 1831.

175. Quoted by Liszt, in Waters, Frederic Chopin, 84.

176. Letter to Ludwika Jedrzejewicz, Paris, February 10, 1848.

177. Letter to his Family, Paris, February 11, 1848.

Tomorrow I go to Edinburgh and perhaps I may even be heard there. But don't suppose that this will give, apart from the occupation, anything except impatience and exhaustion. Still, I find many person here who appear to care for music. They torment me to play and out of politeness I play, always with a fresh regret, swearing that no one will catch me again.[178]

178. Letter to Mlle de Rozieres, Keir, October 20, 1848.

1849

I play less and less ...[179]

179. Letter to Wojciech Grzymala, Paris, July 10, 1849.

Chopin on Teaching

1831

I cannot bear to hear the doorbell. Some person in whiskers, huge, tall, superb, comes in, sits down to the piano and improvises he doesn't know what, bangs and pounds without any meaning, throws himself about, crosses his hands, clatters on one key for five minutes with an enormous thumb that once belonged in the Ukraina holding the reins or wielding a bailiff's cudgel. Here you have a portrait of Sowinski. If ever I have seen a better picture of charlatanism or stupidity in art, it is now. My ears burn, I could fling him out of doors, but I must spare his feelings.[180]

180. Letter to Tytus Wojciechowski, Paris, December 25, 1831.

1832

The pupils of the Conservatoire, Moschele's pupils, those of Herz and Kalkbrenner, in a word finished artists, take lessons from me.

I have five lessons to give today. You think I am making a fortune? Carriages and white gloves cost more and without them one would not be in good taste.[181]

181. Letter to Dominik Dziewanowski, Paris, 1832.

1836

Why must it be twelve already? At twelve I have to give a lesson and to keep on till six o'clock.[182]

182. Letter to Teresa Wodzinska, Paris, November 1, 1836.

I must sit like a stone till five o'clock, giving lessons (just finishing the second one). God knows what will come of it.[182-A]

182-A. Letter to Wojciech Grzymala, Paris, Undated

1844

My lessons are not yet started. Primo: I have only just received a piano. Secundo: People here don't know yet that I have arrived. It will come little by little; I am not anxious.[183]

183.   Letter to George Sand, Paris, December 5, 1844.

1846

It will soon be time to think of the treadmill, that is, the lessons.[184]

184.   Letter to his Family, Nohant, October 11, 1846.

1847

Yesterday I had to give seven lessons. Today I have to give a lesson to young Mme Rothschild, then to a lady from Marseilles, then to an English woman, then to a Swedish one.[185]

185.   Letter to his Family, Paris, April 19, 1847.

1848

Here and there I am beginning to get a reputation, but it needs time. But what is not so plentiful as they say, is money. There's a great deal of lying; directly they don't want anything, they have gone into the country. One lady pupil of mine has gone into the country without paying for nine lessons. Others, who are supposed to take two lessons a week, usually miss both; so there is more pretense than fact. I am not surprised because they are trying to do too much all around. One pupil came here from Liverpool for a week! I gave her five lessons, as they don't play on Sunday, and she is satisfied. Lady Peel, for instance, wants me to give lessons to her daughter who has a great deal of ability, but as she has had a teacher who took half a guinea twice a week, she wants me to give only one lesson a week so that the effect on her purse shall be the same. This is to be able to say that she is having lessons from me, and she will probably leave town in two weeks.[186]

186.   Letter to Wojciech Grzymala, London, July, 1848.

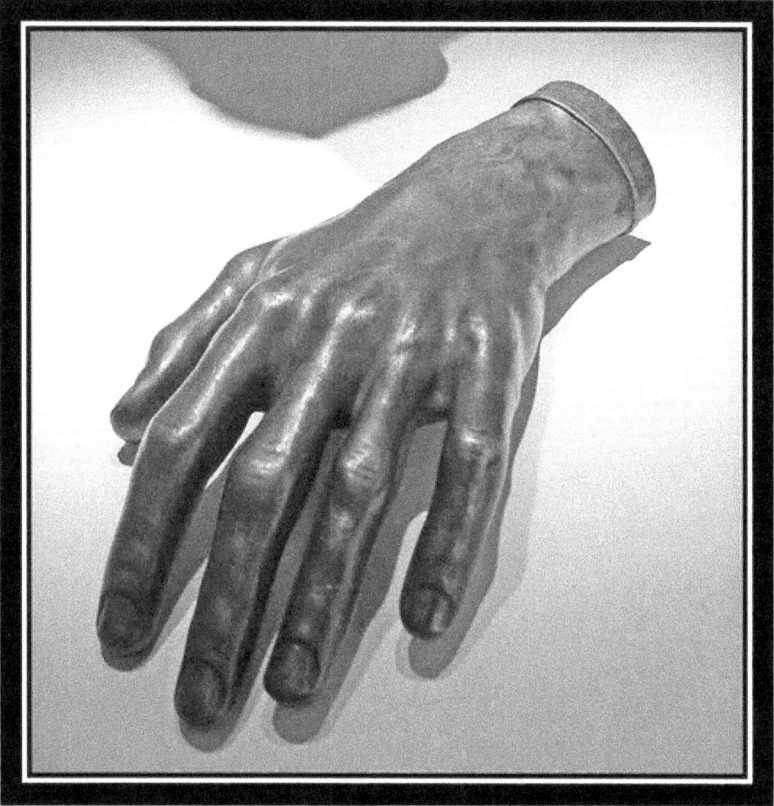

Part 2

Chopin's View
of the World of Music

CHAPTER SEVEN

Chopin's Observations on Performance

On Pianoforte Playing

1825

A certain Mr. Rembielinski, a nephew of the President, has come to Warsaw from Paris. He has been there six years and plays the piano as I have never yet heard it played. You can imagine what a joy that is for us, who never hear anything of real excellence here. He is not appearing as an Artist, but as an Amateur. I won't go into detail about his quick, smooth, rounded playing; I will only tell you that his left hand is as strong as the right, which is an unusual thing to find in one person.[187]

187.   Letter to Jan Bialoblocki, Warsaw, October 30, 1825.

1830

Young Leszkiewicz plays very well, but still chiefly from the elbow.[188]

188.   Letter to Tytus Wojciechowski, Warsaw, April 10, 1830.

Wörlitzer, pianist to His Majesty the King of Prussia, has been here for two weeks. He plays excellently. He's a little Jew, very intelligent by nature and has played us several things which he has learned very thoroughly … He's really only a child still, at sixteen. His forte is the Moscheles Variations on Alexander's March. He plays them splendidly; I think there is nothing lacking. You will be pleased with his playing, although between ourselves he is not up to the title that he bears …

There is also a Frenchman here, a M. Standt. He thought of giving a concert, came to me, reconsidered the matter and gave it up.[189]

189.   Letter to Tytus Wojciechowski, Warsaw, May 15, 1830.

There is a certain Mlle Belleville here, a French woman, who plays the piano very well, most lightly and elegantly, ten times better than Wörlitzer.[190]

190.   Letter to Tytus Wojciechowski, Warsaw, June 5, 1830.

As for Thalberg, he plays excellently but he's not my man. Younger than I, pleases the ladies, makes potpourris … gets his piano by the pedal, not the hand, takes tenths as easily as I octaves, has diamond shirt-studs, does not admire Moscheles, so don't be surprised that only the tutti of my concerto pleased him.[191]

191. Letter to Jan Matuszynski, Vienna, December 25, 1830.

1831

Herz is to play his own Variations on Polish tunes. Poor Polish tunes! You don't know with what Jewish ceremonial music you are to be bombarded, to entice the public by calling it Polish music. After that, try to defend Polish music, express any opinion about it, and you'll be taken for crazy, all the more as Czerny, Vienna's oracle in the manufacture of musical taste, has never yet used a Polish melody for variations.[192]

192.   Letter to his Family, Vienna, May 28, 1831.

I am in very close relations with Kalkbrenner, the first pianist of Europe, whom I think you would like. He is one whose shoe-latchet I am not worthy to untie. Those Herzes, and so on, I tell you they are just windbags and will never play any better.[193]

193.   Letter to K. Kumelski, Paris, September 18, 1831.

I don't know where there can be so many pianists as in Paris, so many asses and so many virtuosi … You would not believe how curious I was about Herz, Liszt, Hiller, etc., — they are all zero beside Kalkbrenner. I confess that I have played like Herz, but would wish to play like Kalkbrenner. If Paganini is perfection, Kalkbrenner is his equal, but in quite another style. It is hard to describe to you his calm, his enchanting touch, his incomparable evenness and the mastery that is displayed in every note. He is a giant walking over Herz and Czerny and all — and over me … I was still more pleased when Kalkbrenner, sitting down to the piano and wanting to do his best before me, made a mistake and had to break off! But you should have heard it when he started again. I had not dreamed of anything like it …

You must know that Kalkbrenner's person is as much hated here as his talent is respected by all. He does not make friends with every fool and, believe me, he is superior to everything that I have heard.[194]

194.   Letter to Tytus Wojciechowski, Paris, December 12, 1831.

On other Instrumentalists

1825

A certain Pan Zak, from the Prague Conservatory, played the clarinet as I have never before heard it played. It will be enough if I tell you that he gets two notes at once with a single breath.[195]

195.   Letter to Jan Bialoblocki, Zelazowa Wola, December 24, 1825.

1830

I am just back from Slawik's — a famous violinist with whom I have made friends. Since Paganini I have heard nothing like him; he can take 96 notes staccato on one bow … incredible.[196]

196.   Letter to Jan Matuszynski, Vienna, December 25, 1830.

1831

Slavik is one of the few local artists whom I enjoy and with whom I get on. He played like another Paganini, but a rejuvenated Paganini, sometimes surpassing the first one. I would not have believed it if I had not heard him often … He strikes his hearers dumb, he make people weep; more, he makes tigers weep, for prince G. and Iskar. Went away moved.[197]

197.   Letter to his Family, Vienna, May 28, 1831.

On Opera and Singers

1828

It happened that I came to Warsaw from Sanniki for a few days just then with Kostus. I was extremely anxious to see *The Barber*. I rubbed my hands for joy all day long. But in the evening, if it hadn't been for Tusa, I should have murdered Colli. He was such an Arlechino Italiano, and so out of tune, that it was abominable. Oh, shame! The Barber went disgracefully.

It is said that *Die Freischütz* was abominably given yesterday. The choir singers were a beat behind each other.[198]

198.   Letter to Tytus Wojciechowski, Warsaw, September 9, 1828.

1830

You can't think how delightful it was to meet Sonntag more intimately, just in the house, on a sofa. You know we think of

nothing but this messenger of God, as some enthusiasts here
have named her … During the week that she has been here,
I have not profited much by the acquaintance, as I saw that
she was worn out by incredibly dull visitors: governors of
fortresses, generals, senators and adjutants, who just sat there
gaping at her and talking about the weather. She receives them
all most courteously; she is too kind-hearted for anything
else …

Sonntag is not beautiful, but extraordinarily pretty. She
charms everyone with her voice, which is not very big…but is
very highly cultivated. Her diminuendi are non plus ultra, her
portamenti lively and especially her ascending chromatic scales
are exquisite. She sang for us Mercadante's aria very, very, very
beautifully. [She also sang] Rode's Variations, the last of which
was particularly good; the Variations on Swiss themes were
so much admired that, when recalled, instead of bowing to
express her thanks, she sang them over again! She is incredibly
good-natured. Yesterday the same thing happened with
Rode's variations. She sang us the Cavatina from the Barber,
the famous one, and from *La Gazza Ladra*. You can imagine
what a difference from everything that you have ever heard …
I met Soliwa and the girls there: I heard them sing that duet
of his. Sonntag told them that their voices are strained; that
their method is good but that they must produce their voices
differently if they don't want to lose them altogether in two
years … Sonntag's style is a supernatural amiability; it is
coquetry, carried to such a point that it becomes natural; it is
impossible to suppose that anyone could be like that by nature,
without knowing the resources of coquetry.

She uses a few embroideries of a quite new type, which
produce an immense effect, though less than those of
Paganini, perhaps because the type is slighter. It seems as if
she breathed some perfume of the freshest flowers into the
hall. She caresses, she strokes, she enraptures but she seldom
moves to tears. Though Radziwill told me she so acts and sings
Desdemona's last scene with Othello that no one can refrain
from weeping.

Her concerts are short: usually she sings four times, and no one plays between except the orchestra. And really her singing is so exciting that one needs a rest after it.[199]

199.　Letter to Tytus Wojciechowski, Warsaw, June 5, 1830.

Gladkowska does not lack much; better on the stage than in a hall. Quite apart from the tragic acting — splendid, nothing to be said about that — the singing itself, if it weren't for the F sharp, and G, sometimes in the high register one could not ask for anything better of its kind. As for her phrasing, it would delight you; she shades gorgeously, and though on first entering her voice shook a little, afterwards she sang very bravely.

[Regarding other members of the cast] Szczurowski is dreadful; scraps of Talma, Kemple, Devrient and Zolkowski in turn; you can't make anything of it, he's perfectly cracked. Salomonowicz is unfortunate: Nawrocka drawls continually and Zylinski digests his dinner on the stage.[200]

200.　Letter to Tytus Wojciechowski, Warsaw, August 21, 1830

There won't be a second Gladkowska, as regards purity and intonation and higher emotions, as they are understood on the stage.[201]

201.　Letter to Tytus Wojciechowski, Warsaw, August 31, 1830.

After dinner came Wild, a famous — perhaps today the most famous — German tenor. I accompanied him from memory in the aria from Othello, which he sang like a master. He and Hinefetter support the entire opera here; it is true it is a miserable one, quite unworthy of Vienna. Fräulein Heinfetter is almost completely lacking in feeling, a voice such as I do not often hear. Everything sung well, every note accurately performed, purity, flexibility, portamenta — but so cold that I almost got my nose frostbitten while sitting in the front row near the stage.[202]

202.　Letter to Jan Matuszynski, Vienna, December 25, 1830.

1831

I had never really heard the Barber till last week in Paris with Lablance, Rubini and Malibran (Garcia). Nor had I heard Othello till I heard it with Rubini, Pasta and Lablanche, nor the Italian in Algers, till I heard it with Rubini, Lablache and Mme. Raimbeaux. If ever I had everything at once, it's now, in Paris. You can't conceive what Lablance is like! Pasta is said to have gone off somewhat, but I have seen nothing more exalted. Malibran depends only on her marvelous voice, no one sings like her! Wonderful, wonderful! Rubini is a splendid tenor and takes his notes authentically, not in falsetto, and sometimes sings roulades for two hours together. Sometimes he embroiders too much and makes his voice tremble purposely; also he continually trills, which, however, brings him more applause than all else. His mezza voce is incomparable. Schröder-Devrient is here; but does not produce such a furore as in Germany.

Mme Cinti-Damoreau sings as superbly as possible; I prefer her singing to Malibran's. Malibran amazes, Cinti delights, and her chromatic scales are better than those of Toulon the famous flautist. No voice could be more highly trained. It seems to cost her so little to sing, as if she just blew it at the audience. Nourrit, the French tenor, has wonderful feeling! And Cholet … is … tantalizing, marvelous, a genius with the real voice of romance.[203]

203.   Letter to Tytus Wojciechowski, Paris, December 12, 1831.

Lablache, Rubini, Passta, Malibran, Devrient, Schröder, Santini and others enchant us three times a week on a grand scale. Nourrit, Levasseur, Derivis, Mme Cinti-Damoreau, Mlle Dorus sustain grand opera; Cholet, Mlle Casimir, Prevost are admirable in comic opera. In a word, here for the first time one can learn what singing is. Certainly today, not Pasta but Maibran is the first singer of Europe — marvelous![204]

204.   Letter to Joseph Elsner, Paris, December 14, 1831.

On Ensembles

1830

The day before yesterday I went for the second time to General Szembek's camp … He ordered his band to perform, they had been practicing all the morning and I heard some remarkable things. It's all on trumpets: a kind called Bugle. You would not believe that they can do chromatic scales, extremely fast, and diminuendo ascending. I had to praise the soloist; poor chap, he doubtless was greatly impressed when I heard the Cavatina from *La Muette de Portici* played on these trumpets with the utmost accuracy and delicate shading.[205]

205.   Letter to Tytus Wojciechowski, Warsaw, August 31, 1830.

1831

Three orchestras in Paris, the Academy, the Italian and Fedau's, are splendid.[206]

206. Letter to Joseph Elsner , Paris, December 14, 1831.

CHAPTER EIGHT

Chopin's Views on Criticism

1828

The pianist Sowinski has written a few words to me, saying that before he comes to Warsaw he would like to know me in advance by correspondence. As he is on the editorial staff of the Parisian periodical, *Revue Musicale*, he would be glad to have some information about the state of music in Poland, about what prominent Polish musicians there are, about their lives, etc. I'm not going to mix up with it. I shall write to him from Berlin that I don't undertake such things.

I have not yet judgment enough for a leading Parisian paper, which must publish only the truth. I should hurt many people's feelings![207]

207. Letter to Tytus Wojciechowski, Warsaw, September 9, 1828.

1830

I feel, more than ever before, that the man has not been born who can please everyone.[208]

208. Letter to Tytus Wojciechowski, Warsaw, March 27, 1830.

I don't want to read anything more that people write about me, or to hear anything they say.[209]

209. Letter to Tytus Wojciechowski, Warsaw, April 17, 1830.

Würfel continues to bombard me about a concert, saying that the local papers have written a lot about my F minor Concerto; as to which I do not know and have had no curiosity to find out.[210]

210. Letter to his Family, Vienna, December 1, 1830.

CHAPTER NINE

Chopin's Views on Places and Peoples

Italy

1830

My head aches when I think of Italy.[211]

211. Letter to Tytus Wojciechowski, Warsaw, August 31, 1830.

London

1848

Well, at last I am installed in the abyss that is called London.[212]

212. Letter to Adolf Gutman, London, May 6, 1848.

I have been offered the Philharmonic, but don't want to play there because it would be with the orchestra. I have been there to observe. Prudent played his concerto and it was a fiasco. There one must play Beethoven, Mozart or Mendelssohn. Although, the directors and others tell me that my concerti have already been played there, and with success, I prefer not to try for it may come to nothing. The orchestra is like their roast beef or their turtle soup: excellent, strong but nothing more. All that I have written is needless as an excuse; there is one impossible thing: they never rehearse, for everyone's time is dear nowadays. There is only one rehearsal, and that is public.[213]

213. Letter to Wojciech Crzymala, London, May 13, 1848.

I see that people are not so open-handed here and that difficulties over money exist everywhere. For the bourgeois class one must do something startling, mechanical, of which I am not capable. The upper world, which travels, is proud, cultivated and just when they are minded to examine anything. But, so much distracted by thousands of things, so

surrounded by the boredom of conventionalities, that it is all
one to them whether music is good or bad, since they have
to hear it from morning till night. For here they have flower-
shows with music, dinners with music, sales with music.[214]

214.   Letter to Wojciech Grzymala,
London, June 2, 1848.

Here, whatever is not boring, is not English.[215]

215.   Letter to Wojciech Grzymala,
London, Juy 8–17, 1848.

If only London were not so dark, and the people so heavy,
and if there were no fogs or smells of soot, I would have
learned English by now. But these English are so different from
the French, to whom I have grown attached as to my own.
They think only in terms of money; they like art because it is
a luxury; kind-hearted, but so eccentric that I understand how
one can himself grow stiff here, or turn into a machine.[216]

216.   Letter to his Family,
August 19, 1848.

Art, here, means painting, sculpture and architecture.
Music is not art and is not called art. If you say an artist, an
Englishman understands that as meaning a painter, architect
or sculptor. Music is a profession, not an art and no one speaks
or writes of any musician as an artist. In their language and
customs it is something else than art; it is a profession. Ask any
Englishman and he will tell you so ...

These queer folk play for the sake of beauty, but to teach
them decent things is a joke. Lady ___, one of the first great
ladies here, in whose castle I spent a few days, is regarded here
as a great musician. One day, after my piano ..., they brought
a kind of accordion and she began with the utmost gravity
to play on it the most atrocious tunes ... Every creature here
seems to me to have a screw loose ... Another sang, standing
up for the sake of originality, and accompanying herself on
the piano, a French-English romance, I am loved. The Princess
of Parma told me that one lady whistled for her with a guitar
accompaniment. Every observation ends with, 'like water,'
meaning that it flows like water. I have not yet played to any
English woman without her saying to me, 'Like Water!' They
all look at their hands and play the wrong notes with much
feeling. Eccentric folk, God help them.[217]

217.   Letter to Wojciech Grzymala,
Scotland, October 21, 1848.

On Thursday at this hour I leave this beastly London. One
more day here and I should not die, but go mad.[218]

218.   Letter to Wojciech Grzymala,
London, November, 1848.

Paris

1831

Every Frenchman dances and shouts, even if his bones are bare. I arrived here fairly comfortably and am glad that I am remaining here. I have the first musicians in the world and the first opera in the world. I know Rossini, Cherubini, Paer, etc., and perhaps may stay longer than I intended. Not because I am getting on any too well here, but because with time I may get on well. But you need luck …

In Paris there is the utmost luxury, the utmost swinishness, the utmost virtue, the utmost ostentation — but also disease, shouting, racket, bustle and more mud than it is possible to imagine. One can perish in this paradise and it is convenient from this point of view, that nobody asks how anybody lives. You can walk in the streets in winter, dressed in rags and frequent tip-top society. One day you can eat the most hearty dinner for 32 sous in a restaurant with mirrors, gildings and gas lighting and the next you can lunch where they will give you enough for a dickey-bird to eat and charge three times as much. That happened to me before I had paid the necessary tax on ignorance …

What a lot of charitable ladies! They just run after people. Nevertheless there is no lack whatsoever of hefty sharks.[219]

219.   Letter to K. Kumelski, Paris, September 18, 1831.

Paris is whatever you choose. You can amuse yourself, be bored, laugh, cry, do anything you like. Nobody looks at you because thousands of others are doing the same as you, and everyone goes his own road. I don't know where there can be so many pianists as in Paris, so many asses and so many virtuosi.[220]

220.   Letter to Tytus Wojciechowski, Paris, December 12, 1831.

This is a queer people; as soon as evening comes you hear nothing but voices calling out the titles of new pulp fiction. Sometimes you can buy three, four sheets of rubbish for a sou. It is, 'The art of having lovers and keeping them,' 'The love affairs of priests,' 'The archbishop of Paris with the Duchess du Barry,' and a thousand other such indecencies, sometimes very wittily written.

It is really wonderful to see the methods people hit on here to earn a few pennies. You know that there is great distress here: he exchange is bad, and you can often meet ragged folk with important faces and sometimes you can hear menacing remarks about the stupid Philippe who just hangs on by means of his ministers.

The lower class is thoroughly exasperated and would be glad at any moment to change the character of their misery, but unfortunately the government has taken too many precautions in this matter. So soon as the smallest street crows collect, they are dispersed by mounted police.[221]

221.   Letter to Tytus Wojciechowski, Paris, December 25, 1831.

1837

When all around is trouble and disturbance, nobody worries here. Weddings, balls and festivities are so gay that they end by trampling each other. At the fireworks on the Champs de Mars nearly twenty persons paid for their curiosity with their lives in the crush.[222]

222.   Letter to Teresa Wodzinska, Paris, June 18, 1837.

1840

The Conservatoire Orchestra lives on old symphonies which it knows by heart and the public is lucky if it sometimes gets a change to hear a bit of Handel or Bach. Handel has only just begun to be appreciated last year, and even then only through excerpts, not whole works. Thus, last winter a chorus from Judas Maccabeus was performed several times, also a chorus of Bach, I don't know which. Since I have been here, except for Beethoven's Jesus on the Mount of Olives, which I have heard only once, no long great work has been given. Many novelties are tried through at the Concervatoire rehearsals, but there is such a spirit here that no one wants to perform any big works except those of the dead. Therefore we shall not hear at present either Mendelssohn or Schneider or Spohr, or Neukomm, or you. If Cherubini were not at the head of the Conservatoire he too would not be played.[223]

223.   Letter to Jozef Elsner, Paris, July 24, 1840.

1845

All the Protestant families keep Christmas Eve, but most Parisians make no difference between today and yesterday.[224]

224.   Letter to his Family, Paris, October 12, 1845.

1849

Paris is frightful. Thirty-six kinds of weather, plenty of mud, draughts in the room. Nothing goes, for the moment, everything is disgusting.[225]

The cholera is abating, but according to what I am told Paris is becoming more and more deserted. It is hot here and dusty. There is poverty, and dirt, and one sees faces that belong to the other world.[226]

Scotland

1848

The population here is ugly, but apparently good-natured. On the other hand the cows are magnificent, but apparently inclined to gore people.[227]

Vienna

1829

Whoever hears me tells me to play in public … They assure me that now is the most favorable time, because the Viennese are hungry for new music …

I have seen three operas. The orchestra and choir are splendid.[228]

Vienna so overwhelmed, stupefied and hallucinated me.[229]

1830

Somehow or other I must leave all my treasures before Michaelmas and get to Vienna, condemned to perpetual sighing.[230]

Among the numerous pleasures of Vienna the hotel evenings are famous. During supper Strauss or Lanner play waltzes … After every waltz they get huge applause and if they play a Quodlibet, or a fragment of opera, song and dance, the hearers are so overjoyed that they don't know what to do with themselves. It shows the corrupt taste of the Viennese public.[231]

225. Letter to Solange Clesinger, Paris, April 13, 1849.

226. Letter to Solange Clesinger, Paris, July 4, 1849.

227. Letter to Auguste Franchomme, Edinburgh, August 6, 1848.

228. Letter to his Family, Vienna, August 8, 1929.

229. Letter to Tytus Wojciechowski, Warsaw, September 12, 1829.

230. Letter to Tytus Wojciechowski, Warsaw, September 4, 1830.

231. Letter to his Family, Vienna, December, 1830.

I strolled along slowly alone, and at midnight went into St. Stefan's. When I entered there was no one there. Not to hear the mass, but just to look at the huge building at that hour, I got into the darkest corner at the foot of a Gothic pillar. I can't describe the greatness, the magnificence of those huge arches. It was quiet; now and then the footsteps of a sacristan lighting candles at the back of the sanctuary would break in on my lethargy. A coffin behind me, a coffin under me — only the coffin above me was lacking. A mournful harmony all around — I never felt my loneliness so clearly. I loved to drink in this great sight until people and lights began to appear.

I passed through the finest streets of Vienna, not alone now but in the company of a cheerful crowd and reached the castle, where I heard three numbers of a not very good mass, sleepily sung.[232]

232.   Letter to Jan Matuszynski, Vienna, December 25, 1830.

1831

Certainly the opera is good. Wild and Heinefetter delight the local public, but it is a pity that Duport puts on few new things and cares more for his pocket than for the opera. Abbé Stadler regrets this and says it is no longer the old Vienna …

Here waltzes are called compositions! And Strauss and Lanner, who play them for dancing, are called Kapellmeistern. This does not mean that everyone thinks like that, indeed nearly everyone laughs about it. But only waltzes get published.[233]

233.   Letter to Joseph Elsner, Vienna, January 26, 1831.

The people here are not my people. They are kind, but kind from habit. They do everything too respectable, flatly, moderately.[234]

234.   Chopin's diary, Vienna, Spring, 1831.

Yesterday I went to the imperial library with Kandler. You must know that I have long wished to acquaint myself with what is perhaps the richest collection of old musical manuscripts, but I never got around to it. I don't know whether the Bologna library is kept in better and more systematic order, but imagine my astonishment when among the manuscripts I see a book in a case with the name, Chopin. Rather thick and in a good binding. I think: I never heard of any other Chopin. There was a Champin, so I supposed it might he his name misspelt, or some such thing. I take it up, look – my hand. Haslinger has presented the manuscript of my Variations to the library. 'Wow,' I say to myself, 'you have found something to keep!'[235]

235.   Letter to his Family, Vienna, May 14, 1831.

People here are terribly frightened of cholera; you can't help laughing. They are selling printed prayers against cholera, they won't eat fruit and most of them are fleeing from town.[236]

236.   Letter to his Family, Vienna, May 28, 1831.

Warsaw

1826

There is a lot said about Freischütz being given in two or three weeks; it seems to me it will make quite a noise in Warsaw. Apparently there will be many performances and that is right. It certainly is much if our opera can manage to give Weber's splendid work. But considering the aim towards which Weber was striving in the Freischütz, his German origin, that strange romanticism and the extremely subtle harmony, peculiarly suited to German taste, one may gather that the Warsaw public, accustomed to Rossini's light style, is likely at first to praise it not from conviction but just in accordance with expert opinion, because Weber is praised everywhere.[237]

237.   Letter to Jan Bialoblocki, Warsaw, August 31, 1830.

1830

Rossini makes more impression on our public, especially when it is also charmed by the garments of a young girl and by what is under the garments, than all the complaints of an unhappy daughter or the most beautiful exaltations of Paer.[238]

238.   Letter to Tytus Wojciechowski, Warsaw, August 31, 1830.

Bach

1839

Having nothing to do, I am correcting the Paris edition of Bach, not only the engraver's mistakes, but also the mistakes hallowed by those who are supposed to understand Bach. I have no pretensions to understand better, but I do think that sometimes I can guess.[239]

239.   Letter to Juljan Fontana, Nohant, August, 1839.

Balfe

1845

Today is to be the fist performance of the Grand Opera of an opera by Balfe ... People don't expect much of it.

Since I wrote the last line, I have been to Balfe's opera. It is not good at all.[240]

240.   Letter to his Family, Paris, October 12, 1845.

Beethoven

1829

I haven't heard anything so great as Beethoven's last quartet for a long time. Beethoven snaps his fingers at the whole world.[241]

241.   Letter to Tytus Wojciechowski, Warsaw, October 20, 1829.

Czerny

1829

Czerny is more sensitive than any of his compositions.[242]

242.   Letter to his Family, August 19, 1829.

I have made close friends with Czerny; we often played together on two pianofortes at his house. He's a good fellow, but nothing more.[243]

243.   Letter to Tytus Wojciechowski, Warsaw, September 12, 1829.

1830

Czerny, on whom I have already called (humbly as always and with everybody), asked me what I 'hat fleissig studiert?' He has again arranged some overture for eight pianos and sixteen players and is quite pleased.[244]

244.   Letter to his Family, Vienna, December 1, 1830.

1831

Czerny, Vienna's oracle in the manufacture of musical taste ...[245]

245.   Letter to his Family, Vienna, July, 1831.

Ferdinand David

1845

I am glad you will hear David's symphony, Le Desert. Except for a few genuine Arabian songs, the only merit of the rest is the orchestration.[246]

246.   Letter to his Family, Nohant, October 1, 1845.

1847

David's 'Christopher Columbus' has almost as great a success as The Desert. I have not heard it … and I don't feel impatient to hear it.[247]

247.   Letter to his Family, Paris, April 19, 1847.

Dalacroix

1845

He is the most admirable artist that one could meet. I have spent delightful hours in his house. He adores Mozart and knows all his operas by heart.[248]

248.   Letter to Auguste Franchomme, Nohant, August 30, 1845.

Gossec

1847

Gossec was a well known and respected French composer at the end of the last century. In the choruses to his Athalie (which are fairly dull) it has been customary of late to play at the end a very beautiful chorus from Haydn's Creation. When Gossec was very old, about 35 years ago, hearing this he remarked quite naively, 'I have no recollection of having written that.'[249]

249.   Letter to his Family, Paris, April 19, 1847.

Handel

1828

Handel's Oratorio, Cacilienfest, is nearer to the ideal that I have formed of great music.[250]

250.   Letter to his Family, Berlin, September 20, 1828.

Hiller

1831

Hiller is an immensely talented fellow (a former pupil of Hummel) whose Concerto and Symphony produced a great affect three days ago. He's on the same lines as Beethoven, but a man full of poetry, fire and spirit.[251]

251.   Letter to Tytus Wojcidchowski, Paris, December 12, 1831.

Victor Hugo

1845

M. Billard, a historical painter, not specially famous, and an ugly man, had a pretty wife whom Hugo seduced. When M. Billard surprised his wife with the poet, so that Hugo was obliged, as the man wanted to arrest him, to show his medal of a peer of France, in order to gain a moment's respite. M. Billard wanted to bring an action against his wife, but it ended in a private separation. Hugo suddenly started off for a several month's trip and Mme Hugo has taken Mme Billard under her protection. Juliette, an actress who has been famous here for ten years and whom Hugo has long been keeping, in spite of Mme Hugo and his children and his poems on family morality, this Juliette has gone with him. Parisian tongues are glad to have something to wag about and it is a funny story. Add to it that Hugo is getting on toward fifty years of age and always, on every occasion, plays the part of a serious person, superior to everyone.[252]

252. Letter to his Family, Nohant, July 20, 1845.

Hummel

1830

Yesterday morning Hummel came to me with his son, who is finishing my portrait. Old Hummel is kindness itself.[253]

253. Letter to his Family, Vienna, December, 1830.

Lesueur

1845

Lesueur is also to have a monument in his native town, Abbeville. Lesueur was Napoleon's music director, a member of the Institute and a professor in the Conservatoire. He was a worthy and enlightened man.[254]

254. Letter to his Family, Nohant, July 20, 1845.

Jenny Lind

1848

I heard Miss Lind in the Sonnambula. It was very beautiful.[255]

255. Letter to Adolf Gutman, London, May 6, 1848.

She is a typical Swede, not in an ordinary light but in some sort of Polar dawn. She is enormously effective in Sonnambula. She sings with extreme purity and certainty and her piano notes are steady, and as even as a hair.[256]

256. Letter to Wojciech Grzymala, London, May 11, 1848.

Liszt

1833

At this moment Liszt is playing my etudes and transporting me outside of my respectable thoughts. I should like to steal from him the way to play my own etudes.[257]

257. Letter to Ferdinand Hiller, Paris, June 20, 1833.

Upon being told that an article by Liszt would 'make you a beautiful kingdom,' Chopin answered, 'Yes, within his own empire.'[258]

258. Quoted by a contemporary French critic, in Edward N. Waters, Frederic Chopin. London: Collier-Macmillan, 1963, 11.

1841

It's a pity that the Tarantella went to Berlin for, as you saw from Schubert's letter, Liszt is involved in these money affairs and I may have unpleasantness about it. He is a touchy Hungarian and ready to think … that I don't trust him, or something of that sort.[259]

259. Letter to Juljan Fontana, Nohant, August 16, 1841.

He will live to be a deputy or perhaps even a king, in Abyssinia or in the Congo, but as for the themes of his compositions, they will repose in the newspapers …[260]

260. Letter to Juljan Fontana, Nohant, September 13, 1841.

1845

Liszt also called on me; he has separated from Mme Calergis and I see, from my questions, that there has been more talk than fact.[261]

261. Letter to his Family, Paris, October 12, 1845.

Mendelssohn

1848

After my matinees many papers had good criticisms, excepting the Times, in which a certain Davison wrote, 'a creature of poor Mendelssohn.' He does not know me and imagines, I am told, that I am an antagonist of Mendelssohn. It does not matter to me. Only, you see, everywhere in the world people are actuated by something else than Truth.[262]

262. Letter to his Family, August 19, 1848.

Meyerbeer

1931

I don't know whether there has ever been such magnificence in a theater, whether it has ever before attained to the pomp of the new five act opera, Robert le Diable, by Meyerbeer ... It is a masterpiece of the new school, in which devils (huge choirs) sing through speaking-trumpets, and souls rise from graves ... There is a diorama in the theater in which at the end you see the interior of a church, the whole church, at Christmas or Easter, lighted up, with monks and all the congregation on the benches and censors — even with the organ, the sound of which on the stage is enchanting and amazing, also it drowns the orchestra. Nothing of the sort could be put on anywhere else. Meyerbeer has immortalized himself! But he has spent three years in Paris to get it done. It is said he has paid 20,000 francs to the cast.[263]

263.   Letter to Tytus Wojciechowski, Paris, December 12, 1831.

Reicha

1831

Reicha I have merely seen and you know how eager I was to meet that man. Now I know several of his pupils who have given me a different impression of him. He does not care for music, does not even attend the Conservatoire concerts, does not wish to talk of music with anyone, during his lessons looks continually at his watch and so on.

These people, Reicha and Cherubini, are dried up chrysalises whom one can only regard with respect and learn something from their compositions.[264]

264.   Letter to Joseph Elsner, Paris, December 14, 1831.

George Sand

1839

Today she is writing in bed all day. You know, you would love her even more if you knew her as I know her today.[265]

265.   Letter to Wojciech Grzymala, Marseilles, April 12, 1839.

1848

George Sand is putting on a comedy in the village in her daughter's bride-room. She has forgotten herself, is doing crazy things and will not come to her senses until her heart begins to ache badly. At present it is dominated by her head.

I have had my cross to carry. May God pity her, if she can't distinguish between genuine affection and flattery. And yet, perhaps it only appears to me that others are flatterers and perhaps her happiness is really there where I can't see it. Her friends, her neighbors have long understood nothing of what was happening there of late, but now perhaps they are accustomed. For the rest, no one will ever be able to steer through the caprices of such a mind. Eight years of any settled arrangement was too much. God willed just those to be the years in which her children were growing up and if I had not been there I don't know how long ago the children would have been with their father, not with her. Maurice, too, will run away to his father at the first opportunity. But perhaps, after all, those are the conditions of her life, of her literary talent, of her happiness?[266]

266. Letter to Ludwika Jedrzejewicz, Paris, February 10, 1848.

Schubert

The sublime becomes drab when followed by the common or the trivial.[267]

267. Quoted by Liszt, in Waters, Op. cit., 145.

Clara Schumann

1839

If you liked Clara Wieck, you were right; she plays — no one better. If you see her, greet her from me, and her Father too.[268]

268. Letter to Juljan Fontana, Marseilles, March, 1839.

Spohr

1830

Today I played Spohr's Quintetto for piano, clarinet, bassoon, horn and flute. Beautiful, but dreadfully unpianistic. Everything he tried to write to display the piano is insufferable difficult and often you can't find your fingers.[269]

269. Letter to Tytus Wojciechowski, Warsaw, September 18, 1830.

Weber

1826

Weber's splendid composition, Der Freischütz, with that strange romanticism and the extremely subtle harmony, peculiarly suited to German taste.[270]

270.   Letter to Jan Bialoblocki, Warsaw, June, 1826.

Part 3

Chopin's Reflections
on his own Music

CHAPTER TEN

Chopin on his own Musical Studies

1826

I go to Elsner for strict counterpoint, six hours a week.[271]

1829

No one here wants to take me as a pupil. Blahetka said nothing surprised him so much as my having learned all that in Warsaw. I answered that under Zywny and Elsner the greatest donkey could learn.[272]

1830

The Official Bulletin says that if I had fallen into the hands of some pedant or Rossinist — which is a stupid term — I should not have been what I am. I am nothing, but he is right in saying that. If I had not been taught by Elsner, who imbued me with convictions, I should doubtless have accomplished still less than I now have.[273]

1831

Since Kalkbrenner and I meet daily, either he comes to me or I to him. On closer acquaintance he has made me an offer, that I should study with him for three years and he will make something out of me. I answered that I know how much I lack, but that I cannot exploit him and three years is too much.[274]

I know how much I lack and how far I have to go if I am to approach any standard of yours and I still make bold to think: 'At least I shall get a little nearer to him.

To be a great composer one must have enormous knowledge, which, as you have taught me, demands not only listening to the work of others, but still more listening to one's own.

271.   Letter to Jan Bialoblocki, Warsaw, November 2, 1826.

272.   Letter to his Family, Vienna, August 19, 1829.

273.   Letter to Tytus Wojciechowski, Warsaw, April 10, 1830.

274.   Letter to Tytus Wojciechowski, Paris, December 12, 1831.

Here and there in Germany I am known as a pianist.
Certain musical papers have spoken of my concerts, raising
hopes that I shall shortly be seen taking my place among the
first virtuosi of my instrument ... Today only one possibility
offers for the fulfillment of this promise; why should I not
seize it? In Germany I could not have learned the piano from
anyone, for though there were persons who felt that I still lack
something, but no one knew what. Also, I could not see the
beam in my eye which still prevents my looking higher. Three
years of study with Kalkbrenner is a long time, too long.
Even Kalkbrenner admits that, now that he has examined me
more closely ... But I would be willing to stick to it for three
years if that will only enable me to take a big step forward in
what I have undertaken. I understand enough not to become a
copy of Kalkbrenner. Nothing will interfere with my perhaps
overbold, but at least not ignoble, desire to create a new world
for myself. If I work, it is in order to have a firmer standing.[275]

275.   Letter to Joseph Elsner, Paris, December 14, 1831.

Send without fail Cherubini's Treatise on Counterpoint and
Fugue.[276]

276.   Letter to Juljan Fontana, Paris [undated].

CHAPTER ELEVEN

Chopin on his Creative Process

1828

For the last week I have written nothing either for men or for God. I very seldom get an idea like the one that came to my fingers so easily one morning on your piano.[277]

1830

The Rondo of the new concerto is not finished, and for that one must be in the mood. I am not even hurrying with it, because once I've got the opening Allegro I don't worry about the rest.[278]

I have begun a Polonaise with the orchestra, but so far it's just rudiments. It is only a beginning of a beginning.[279]

1831

To be a great composer one must have enormous knowledge, which, as you have taught me, demands not only listening to the work of others, but still more listening to one's own.[280]

1838

I heard only today that the piano was put on a trading vessel in Marseilles on December first ... Meanwhile my manuscripts sleep.[281]

Regardless of my transient joys, I am never free of a feeling of melancholy which somehow forms the base of my heart.[282]

I write because I do so love my laborious writings.[283]

1845

I must finish certain manuscripts before leaving here for I can't compose in winter.[284]

277. Letter to Tytus Wojciechowski, Warsaw, December 27, 1828.

278. Letter to Tytus Wojciechowski, Warsaw, May 15, 1830.

279. Letter to Tytus Wojciechowski, Warsaw, September 18, 1830.

280. Letter to Joseph Elsner, Paris, December 14, 1831.

281. Letter to Juljan Fontana, Palma, December 14, 1838.

282. An answer to a lady who was moved by his playing and questioned him regarding the source of his emotions, quoted by Franz Liszt, in Edward N. Waters, in Frederic Chopin. London: Collier-Macmillan, 1963, 79.

283. Letter to Juljan Fontana [undated].

284. Letter to his Family, Nohant, October 1, 1845.

1846

When one does a thing, it appears good otherwise one would not write it. Only later comes reflection and one discards or accepts the thing. Time is the best censor, and patience a most excellent teacher.[285]

285.   Letter to his Family, Nohant, October 11, 1846.

1848

Of musical ideas there can be no question; I am utterly out of the running and make on myself the impression of an ass at a masquerade, or rather like a violin's E string on a bass viol: astonished, tricked, knocked off balance.[286]

286.   Letter to Auguste Franchomme, Edinburgh, August 6, 1848.

Chapter Twelve

Chopin on his Own Compositions

1830

As I have no established reputation as yet, the musicians here admired and feared to admire; could not make out whether the compositions were good, or whether they only thought they were. One of the local connoisseurs came up to me and praised the novelty of the form; saying that he had never before heard anything in that form. I don't know who he was, but he was perhaps the one who understood me best.[287]

287. Letter to his Family, Breslau, November 9, 1830.

1839

I should very much like to have my preludes dedicated to Pleyel — there's probably still time, as they are not printed. And the Ballade to Robert Schumann. The Polonaises to you, as they are. To Kessler, nothing. If Playel does not want to give up the Ballades, then dedicate the Preludes to Schumann.[288]

288. Letter to Juljan Fontana, Marseilles, Spring, 1839.

You know that I have four new mazurkas: one in C minor, from Palma, three written here, B major, D-flat major and C sharp minor. They seem to me good, as is always he case with younger children, when the parents are growing old.[289]

289. Letter to Juljan Fontana, Nohant, August, 1839.

1843

My manuscripts are worth nothing, but it would mean a lot of work for me if they were lost.[290]

290. Letter to Wojciech Crzymala, Nohant, 1843.

Rondo à la Krakowiak in F major [1828]

1828

The score of the Rondo à Krakowiak is finished. The introduction is original, more so than I myself even in a beige suit. But the Trio is not yet finished.[291]

291. Letter to Tytus Wojciechowski, Warsaw, December 27, 1828.

Introduction and Polonaise in C major [1829–1830]

1929

There is nothing in it but glitter; a salon piece for ladies ...[292]

292. Letter to Tytus Wojciechowski, Warsaw, November 14, 1829.

Variations, 'Souvenir de Paganini' in A major [1829]

1830

The Vienna reviewer says they are short, but so vigorous, so high, so deep and so philosophic as well, that he can't describe them. He ends by saying that, apart from their surface elegance, these Variations have an inner quality which will last. This German has paid me a compliment for which I must thank him when we meet.[293]

293. Letter to Tytus Wojciechowski, Warsaw, September 18, 1830.

Concerto Nr. 1 in E minor [1830]

1830

The Adagio of the new concerto in E minor is not meant to be loud, it's more of a Romance, quiet, melancholy. It should give the impression of gazing tenderly at a place which brings to the mind a thousand dear memories. It is a sort of meditation in beautiful Spring weather, but by moonlight.[294]

The Rondo is effective, the Allegro powerful. Oh, accursed self-love![295]

I think the Rondo will impress everyone.[296]

Etude in G-flat major [1830]

1839

Did Clara Wieck play my etude well? Why could she not choose something better than just the least interesting of the etudes? — at least for those who do not know that it is on the black keys?[297]

Impromptu in F sharp major [1839]

1839

I have my manuscripts in order, properly annotated. There are six of them with your polonaises, not counting the seventh, an Impromptu, which is perhaps poor; I don't know yet, it's too new (yes!).[298]

Tarantella in A-flat major [1841]

1841

I send you the Tartanella. It's a bore for you to copy the beastly thing, but I do hope that it will be a long time before I write anything worse.[299]

294.   Letter to Tytus Wojciechowski, Warsaw, May 15, 1830.

295.   Letter to Tytus Wojciechowski, Warsaw, October 5, 1830.

296.   Letter to Tytus Wojciechowski, Warsaw, October 5, 1830.

297.   Letter to Juljan Fontana, Marseilles, April 25, 1839.

298.   Letter to Juljan Fontana, Nohant, October 10, 1839.

299.   Letter to Juljan Fontana, Paris [undated].

One more worry: at your leisure, copy that wretched Tarantella once more, to send to Wessel as soon as we know the day.[300]

300.   Letter to Juljan Fontana, Nohant, August 16, 1841.

Cello Sonata in G minor [1845–1846]

1846

Sometimes I am satisfied with my violoncello sonatas, sometimes not. I throw it into the corner, then take it up again.[301]

301.   Letter to his Family, Nohant, October 11, 1846.

CHAPTER THIRTEEN

Chopin on the Publishers of his Compositions

1830

Haslinger is shrewd. He wants to put me off, courteously but lightly, so that I may give him my compositions for nothing. Klengel is surprised that he did not pay me for the Variations. Perhaps he thinks that if he appears to have slight regard for my things I shall take it seriously, and give them to him for nothing? 'For nothing' is finished; now Pay, beast![302]

302.   Letter to his Family, Vienna, December 1, 1830.

1839

Get 500 for the ballade from Probst, and then take it to Schlesinger. If I have to deal with Jews, let it at least be Orthodox ones. Probst may swindle me even worse, for he's a sparrow whose tail you can't salt. Schlesinger has always cheated me; but he has made a lot on me, and won't want to refuse another profit; only be polite to him because the Jew likes to pass for somebody.[303]

303.   Letter to Juljan Fontana, Marseilles, March 13, 1839.

Pleyel's a fool and Probst a rascal … No doubt you have received my long letter about Schlesinger. Now I wish, and beg you, give my letter to Pleyel, who finds my manuscripts too dear. If I have to sell them cheap, I would rather let it be to Schlesinger than search for impossible new connections. As Schlesinger can always count on England, and as I am through with Wessel, let him sell them to whom he likes. The same with the Polonaises in Germany, for Probst is a sly bird. I know him of old. Let Schlesinger sell to whom he likes, not necessarily to Probst. It's nothing to me. He adores me, because he's skinning me. Only have a clear understanding with him about the money and don't give up the manuscripts except for cash.

I will send Pleyel a receipt. The fool, can't he trust either me or you? Good Lord, why must one have dealings with scoundrels! That Pleyel, who told me that Schlesinger was underpaying me, and now finds 500 fr. too much for a manuscript for all countries! Well, I prefer to do business with a real Jew. And Probst is a rascal to pay me 300 for the mazurkas! Why, the last mazurkas brought me 800 at the first jump: Probst 300, Schlesinger 400 Wessel 100. I would rather sell my manuscripts for nothing as in the old days, than have to bow and scrape to such fools. And I'd rather be humiliated by one Jew than by three …

Scoundrels, scoundrels.[304]

304.   Letter to Juljan Fontana, Marseilles, March 17, 1839.

Keep my manuscripts so that they may not chance to appear in print before they are given. If the preludes are printed, it's a trick of Probst's … Germans, Jews, rascals, scoundrels, offal, dog-hangers, etc. In short, you can finish the litany, for you know them now as well as I do.[305]

305.   Letter to Juljan Fontana, Marseilles, April 25, 1839.

Wessel is a rogue. I will never send him anything more after the 'Agrements au Salon.' Perhaps you don't know that he has given that title to my second Impromptu, or one of the Waltzes.

Schlesinger needs not complain of my terms, which are very moderate, especially as it is long since I have published anything. All I want is to get out of this position with decency. I know that I am not selling myself. But tell him if I wished to take advantage of him or to cheat him I could write fifteen bad things in a year, which he would buy at 300 and I should have a larger income. Would that me more honest?[306]

306.   Letter to Juljan Fontana [undated].

1843

In the Impromptu which you have issued in the *Gazette municipale* of June 9th, the pages are wrongly numbered, which renders my composition incomprehensible.[307]

307.   Letter to Maurice Schlesinger, Nohant, July 22, 1843.

Appendices

APPENDIX I

Franz Liszt's personal reflections on Chopin

An intelligent analysis of Chopin's works cannot be made without disclosing beauties of a very high order, a wholly new expression, as an harmonic structure as original as it is learned.[1] Here boldness always justifies itself; richness, even exuberance, does not suppress clarity; uniqueness does not sink to baroque eccentricity. The chasings are not undisciplined, and the luxury of ornament does not overburden the elegance of leading lines. His best works abound in combinations which, it may be said, are epoch-making in the treatment of musical style. Daring, brilliant, seductive, they conceal their depth beneath so much grace, their skill beneath so much charm that it is difficult to withdraw sufficiently from their captive hold to judge them coolly from the standpoint of theoretic value. The latter has already been sensed, but it will be increasingly recognized when the time comes for a careful examination of the services rendered to art during the period when Chopin was active.

We owe to him the extension of chords, be they stuck together, arpeggiated or rolled; those chromatic and enharmonic twisting lines, of which his pages offer such striking examples; those little groups of embellishing notes, over the melodic figure, that fall like drops of iridescent dew. He gave to this type of ornament, originating solely in the fioritures of the great and venerated school of Italian song, the elements of surprise and variety beyond the capacity of the human voice which, until then, had been slavishly imitated by the piano in stereotyped and monotonous decoration. He invented those admirable harmonic progressions that lent a serious stamp even to pages seeming to have no claim to such importance because of the lightness of their subject. But

[1]   This material is taken from Franz Liszt, Frederic Chopin. Translated by Edward N. Waters. London: Collier-Macmillan Ltd, 1963, 33ff, 40ff, 81, 83ff, 107ff, 141 and 145.

what matters the subject? Is it not, rather, its flashing idea, its pulsating emotion, that heightens, ennobles and augments if?

•••

Chopin's weak and sickly constitution prevented the vigorous expression of his passions, which he revealed to his friends only as gentle and affectionate. In the bustling, preoccupied world of great cities, where no one has leisure to guess the riddle of another's destiny, where each is judged only by his outward activity, surely very few think it worth while to explore beneath the surface of personal traits. But those who came close to Chopin in intimate and frequent relations had occasion to notice, sometimes, the impatience and vexation he felt at so promptly being taken literally. And the artist could not avenge the man! Too feeble in health to betray this impatience through the vehemence of his own playing, he sought compensation by writing pages that he loved to hear performed with the vigor that he lacked, pages in which swirl the passionate rancors of the man who is more grievously wounded than he is wont to admit.

•••

In his performance Chopin delightfully imparted that sense of restlessness that gave the melody a surging effect, like a skiff on the crest of a mighty wave. Early in his writings he described this style, which lent such an individual stamp to his playing, by the phrase, Tempo rubato: time stolen or broken, a flexible measure, both lingering and abrupt, quivering like a breath-shaken flame. In his later publications he ceased to do this, convinced that if its meanings were understood, it would be impossible to ignore this rule of irregularity. Thus all of his pieces should be played with this measured and accented alternation, the secret of which is difficult to grasp unless he himself was frequently heard. He seemed eager to teach this style to his many students.

•••

Chopin knew, we insist, that he had no effect upon the multitude and could not strike the masses. They are like a sea of lead and no less heavy to move, their waves are stirred by fire. They need the strong arm of the stalwart laborer to be spilled into a mold where the flowing metal suddenly assumes thought and feeling in accordance with the imposed form. He knew that he was completely appreciated only in those too rare gatherings where all the hearers were ready to follow and accompany him into those spheres that the ancients entered solely through an ivory gate surrounded by diamond pilasters crowned by domes, where all prismatic rays play upon a fawny crystal, such as the Mexican opal, its kaleidoscopic foci being hidden in an olive colored mist that covers and discovers them by turns — spheres where all is entrancing magic, mad surprise, dream made manifest, and where Chopin so willingly sought refuse and delight …

Aware of the conditions imposed by the nature of his talent, he played but rarely in public …

We believe that those concerts tired his physical constitution less than they did his artistic sensibility. His voluntary sacrifice of clamorous success concealed, we think, an internal hurt. He had a very clear sense of his great superiority, but perhaps its echo and reverberation did not suffice to bring him the quiet certainty that he was fully appreciated. Popular acclamation was wanting, and he doubtless wondered to what degree the distinguished salons compensated, in the enthusiasm of their applause, for the general public that he avoided … A discontent, perhaps quite indefinite in his mind, at least with respect to its true source, secretly undermined him. He was obviously almost shocked by eulogy. What he was entitled to claim did not arrive in great outburst, and he was inclined to be vexed by isolated praises. He often brushed them off, like annoying dust, with polite remarks, and these made it quickly evident that he felt not only slightly applauded but badly applauded, that he preferred to be undisturbed in his solitude and sentiment.

Much too subtle an expert in jesting and too clever in derision to expose himself to sarcasm, he assumed no attitude of misunderstood genius. Happily complacent in outward appearance, he so completely hid the injury to his rightful pride that its existence was scarcely suspected. But gradually increasing rarity of his concerts could be attributed, not unreasonably, more to his desire to avoid occasions that failed to bring him deserved tributes than to his frailty …

Let us learn from him to cast out all but the noblest ambitions, to concentrate our concerns on efforts that dig a deeper furrow than the fashion of the day!

…

In none of its many manifestations did Chopin's character harbor a single emotion, a single impulse, which was not dictated by the most delicate sense of honor and the noblest understanding of the affections. And yet there never was a nature more inclined to eccentricity, whim, and abrupt caprice. His imagination was passionate, his feelings tended toward violence: his physical system was weak and sickly. Who can measure the sufferings proceeding from such contrasts? They were surely heart-rending, but he never exposed them to view! He kept them hidden, screened from all glances, beneath the impenetrable calm of proud resignation …

Events for him were feelings and impressions, more striking and important than external shifts and happenings. The lessons that he gave, constantly, regularly and assiduously, were his daily and domestic obligation, discharged with satisfaction and in good conscience. He unburdened his soul in compositions as others to in prayer, pouring out those effusions of the heart, those unexpressed sorrows, those indescribable grieves that devout souls spill in their talks with God …

He took part in no activity, no drama, no alliance, no issue. He wielded a decisive influence over no person. His will never encroached upon any desire. He neither fettered nor controlled any mind through the domination of his own. He tyrannized over no heart, he laid no conquering hand on any fate … He also eluded all bonds and all friendships that would have dragged him in their train and thrust him into stormier spheres. Ready to give all, he never gave himself … His closest acquaintances failed to penetrate to that sacred retreat where his soul dwelt, apart from the rest of his life — a retreat so hidden that it was scarce suspected.

In his relations and conversations he appeared concerned only with what interested others; he refrained from imposing his own personality upon theirs. Of the small amount of time he spared them, at least he kept none for himself. Whatever he might have dreamed, whatever he might have wished or wanted or won, whether his white and slender hand could have adapted strings of brass or his lyre's golden cords, no one ever asked him, and in his presence no one would have had opportunity to think thereof. His talk dealt rarely with emotional topics. He glided over them, and since he was ungenerous with his time, his remarks were readily exhausted in the happenings of the day … His whole being was harmonious and seemed to require no comment. The blue of his eye was more animated than dreamy; his fine and gentle smile did not shift to bitterness. The delicacy and transparency of his complexion caught the eye, his blond hair was silky, his nose slightly tilted, his bearing distinguished, and his manner had such an aristocratic stamp that he was instinctively treated like a prince. His gestures were many and graceful, the tone of his voice was always subdued and often dampened, he was small of stature and frail of limb. His entire appearance called to mind the morning-glory, swaying on stems incredibly fine and their cups so divinely colored, but of such a tenuous texture that the least touch would destroy them.

He carried into society the evenness of mood of persons who are undisturbed because they expect no advantage. He was customarily gay. His caustic mind quickly exposed the ridiculous far beyond the surface where it makes its impact. In pantomime he displayed a near inexhaustible comic verve, and he often enjoyed reproducing, in farcical improvisation, the musical mannerisms and special idiosyncrasies of certain virtuosos, repeating their gestures and motions, and mimicking their face with a talent that betrayed their complete personality in a flash …

There were moments, however, admittedly rare, when we caught him very deeply affected. We saw him pale and blanch to such a point that his complexion turned greenish and cadaverous. But in his most violent emotions he retained self-control, and then he was usually reluctant to talk about what he resented …

A Catholic and truly religious, Chopin never approached this subject. He held to his beliefs without parading them. People could know him for a long time and gain no accurate idea of his thoughts on such matters ...

In one field only Chopin abandoned his calculated silence and his customary neutrality. He dropped his reserve in the cause of art. Here alone he would not surrender, under any condition, the explicit declaration of his judgment, and here he persistently endeavored to extend the effect of his influence and his will. This was like the tacit testimony of a great artist's authority which he felt he legitimately held for those questions arising from his skill and calling; and he never left doubt as to how he viewed them. For some years he injected a passionate zeal in his pleadings. Later, since the triumph of his ideas had lessened the interest of his role, he sought no further occasion to assume again the head of any faction ... Keeping free of others in time, thought, and action, he often preferred the company of women, since it involved him less in subsequent relations. He would gladly spend whole evenings playing blind man's buff with young folks, telling them little stories that made them laugh ... He enjoyed the country and life of a chateau. He was ingenious in varying its pleasures and in increasing its cheering events. Moreover, he liked to work there and several of his best compositions, written at such moments, perhaps hold the memory of his happiest days.

...

Chopin will be ranked in the company of the foremost musicians who thus individualized in themselves the poetic sense of a nation, but not only because he chose the rhythm of Polonaises, Mazurkas and Cracoyiennes and called many of his compositions by such names. Had he limited himself to multiplying them, he would only have constantly reproduced the same pattern and the memory of the same experience and deed, a reproduction that would soon have been tedious, serving merely to prolong a form quickly become more or less boring. If his name stands for a poet who is essentially Polish, it is because he used this form solely to express a manner of feeling more prevalent in his country than elsewhere and because the expression of the same emotions occurs in all the forms that he selected. His Preludes, and Etudes, his Nocturnes above all, his Scherzos and Concertos, his shortest compositions as well as the most extended breathe the same type of sensibility expressed in varying degrees, modified and varied in a thousand ways, but always one and unchanging. An eminently subjective composer, Chopin gave to all his works the same vital spark, and he inspirited all of his creations by his own life. Thus all of his works are bound together by a unity, whence it happens that their beauties, like their defects, are always the result of the same order of emotion and a single manner of feeling, a poet's basic requirement for his songs to stir all the hearts of his country to tremble in unison.

…

Everything in Italian music that is simple, glittering and devoid of ornament as of skill; everything in German music that is stamped with vulgar, though powerful, energy displeased him equally … Among composers for the piano, Hummel was the one whom he read again and again with intense pleasure, and in his eyes Mozart was the ideal type, the poet supreme, for more rarely than any other would he deign to cross the step separating the distinctive from the commonplace.

APPENDIX II

George Sand's personal reflections on Chopin

Amantine Lucile Aurore Dupon (1804–1876) was a French novelist who wrote under the pseudonym, George Sand. There are places in her novels where she made a living well-known person, under a different name, a character in her work, presenting the original person is such detail that the result is as valuable as a photograph. Such is the case of her novel, *Lucrezia Floriani* (1847) in which one character is understood to be Chopin. It is all the more valuable as she was the only person who knew him intimately over a period of time.

Gentle, sensitive and exquisite in all things, he had at fifteen years of age all the graces of youth joined to the seriousness of maturity. He remained delicate of body as of mind. But this lack of muscular development meant the retaining of a beauty, an exceptional countenance, that was, so to speak, both ageless and sexless. It was not the bold and masculine appearance of a descendant of that race of ancient magnates who could only drink and hunt and war; neither was it the effeminate sweetness of a rosy cherub. It was something like those idealized creatures that medieval poetry called upon to serve for the adornment of Christian temples. An angel beautiful of face like a sadly noble woman, of pure and slender form like a young god of Olympus, and expression both tender and severe, both chaste and impassioned.

That was the substance of his being. Nothing was purer and, at the same time, more exalted than his thoughts, nothing more constant, more concentrated and more completely devoted than his affections ... But this being understood only what was indistinguishable from himself ... all the rest existed for him only as a kind of vexing dream which he tried to escape from while living in the midst of society. Always lost in his trances, he disliked reality. As a child he could not touch a sharp instrument without being wounded; as an adult he could not face a man different from himself without colliding against this living contradiction …

What saved him from perpetual antagonism was a voluntary and soon inveterate habit of seeing and hearing nothing that generally displeased him, unless it touched his personal affections. Persons who did not think as he did became like phantoms in his eyes, and, since he was charmingly polite, his courteous benevolence could hide from what was only a cold disdain, even as unconquerable aversion …

He never had an hour of expansiveness without paying for it by several hours of withdrawal. The moral causes for this might have been too slight and too subtle to be glimpsed by the naked eye. A microscope would have been needed to read in his soul where so little of the light of the living ever pierced …

It is remarkably strange that, with such a character, he could find any friends. And yet he did have some, not only his mother's, who esteemed him as the worthy son of a noble woman, but also young people of his own age who loved him warmly and were loved by him … He had a high conception of friendship and, in the period of first illusions, he willingly believed that he and his friends, raised in nearly the same manner and on the same principles, would never change opinions and would reach no essential disagreement.

Outwardly he was so affectionate, as a consequence of his fine education and natural grace, that he had the gift of pleasing even those who did not know him. His lovely face spoke in his favor, his physical frailty made him interesting in the eyes of women. The full and flowing culture of his mind, the sweet and pleasant freshness of his words won him the attention of enlightened men. As for those of a coarser mold, they liked his exquisite courtesy, and with their open geniality they responded to it the more since they failed to realize that it was the exercise of a duty with sympathy playing no part.

If these persons could have probed his nature, they would have said he was more friendly than loving, and as far as they were concerned, this would have been true. But how could they have guessed this when his very few attachments were so vital, so deep, and so constant? ...

In ordinary life, association with him was delightful. He practiced all forms of kindness with uncommon graciousness, and in expressing his gratitude he displayed a deep emotion that paid for friendship on usurious terms.

Each day he was prone to believe he was dying, and in this thought he accepted the cares of a friend, concealing from him, however, the shortness of time that he could enjoy his solicitude. He had a great outward courage, and if he did not entertain the thought of approaching death with the heroic jauntiness of youth, at least he savored its expectation with a kind of bitter sensuality.

APPENDIX III

Liszt, on hearing a Recital by Chopin [April 26, 1841]

Last Monday evening at eight o'clock the salons of M. Playel were brilliantly lighted; a ceaseless stream of carriages deposited at the foot of the steps, carpeted and decked with fragrant flowers, the most elegant ladies, the most fashionable young men, the most famous artists, the richest financiers, the most illustrious lords, the elite of society — a complete aristocracy of birth, wealth, talent and beauty.[2]

2   *Revue et Gazette musicale de Paris,* May 2, 1841.

An open grand piano was on a platform; crowding around, people vied for the closest seats; composing themselves in anticipation, they would not miss a chord, a note, an intention, a thought of him who was about to sit there. And they were right to be so greedy, attentive, and religiously wrought up, for the one they waited for, the one they wanted to see, hear, admire and applaud was not only an artist of great renown — he was all this and much more, he was Chopin.

Coming to France some ten years ago Chopin, in the throng of pianists then swarming from everywhere, struggled for neither first nor second place. He was rarely heard in public; the essentially poetic nature of his talent was out of place there. Like those flowers that only release their fragrance in the night, he needed an atmosphere of peace and calm to display the treasure of melody resting in him. Music was his language, the divine language in which he expressed a whole series of feelings that only a few could understand …

With the piano he could not be completely self-revealed. Hence, if we mistake not, a numb and ceaseless suffering, a certain reluctance to outward communication, a sadness concealed beneath a show of gaiety — a complete individuality, indeed, remarkable and engaging to the last degree.

As we have said, only rarely, at very long intervals, was Chopin heard in public. But what would have led any other, almost certainly, to be forgotten and obscured, was exactly what assured him a reputation above the whim of fashion and protected him from rivalries, jealousies and injustice. Chopin, set apart from the violent turmoil that, for some years, thrusts one against or over another, has been steadily surrounded by faithful disciples, enthusiastic pupils and warm friends who, shielding him from vexing clashes and painful contacts, have not ceased to spread his works as well as admiration for his genius and respect for his name. Thus, this celebrity, delicate, high-minded, surpassingly aristocratic, has remained free of all attack. Around him criticism is wholly silent, as if posterity had claimed him ...

Without artificial striving for originality he has been, in his compositions, himself, both in style and conception. To new thoughts he has been able to give new form. The wild and rugged elements of his country have found expression in bold dissonance, in strange harmonies, while the delicacy and grace of his nature are revealed in a thousand turns of phrase, in a thousand ornaments of inimitable imagination ...

Speaking to a society rather than to a public, he could safely show himself as what he is — a poet, elegiac, profound, chaste and dreaming. He had no need to astonish or to shock; he sought delicate sympathy rather than noisy acclaim. Let us say at once that this sympathy was not lacking. With the first chords he established an intimate communication between himself and his audience. Two etudes and a ballade had to be repeated, and but for fear of increasing the fatigue already obviously betrayed in his pale countenance, the crowd would have demanded again every piece on the program.

BIBLIOGRAPHY

Chopin *as revealed by extracts from his diary*. Translated by Natalie Janotha. London, William Reeves, 1906.

Liszt, Franz. *Frédéric Chopin*. Translated by Edward N. Waters. London, Collier-Macmillan, 1963.

Revue et Gazette musicale de Paris [May 2, 1841]

Sand, George. *Lucrezia Floriani* [1847], in Franz Liszt, *Frédéric Chopin*. Paris, Escudier, 1852. Translated by Edward N. Waters. London, Collier-Macmillan, 1963

Voynich, E. L. *Chopin's Letters*. New York, Vienna House, 1973

Waters, Edward N. *Frédéric Chopin*. London, Collier-Macmillan, 1963.

About the author

David Whitwell is a graduate ('with distinction') of the University of Michigan and the Catholic University of America, Washington D.C. (Ph.D., Musicology, Distinguished Alumni Award, 2000) and has studied conducting with Eugene Ormandy and at the Akademie für Musik, Vienna. Prior to coming to Northridge, Dr. Whitwell participated in concerts throughout the United States and Asia as Associate First Horn in the USAF Band and Orchestra in Washington, D.C., and in recitals throughout South America in cooperation with the United States State Department.

At the California State University, Northridge, which is in Los Angeles, Dr. Whitwell developed the CSUN Wind Ensemble into an ensemble of international reputation, with international tours to Europe in 1981 and 1989 and to Japan in 1984. The CSUN Wind Ensemble has made professional studio recordings for BBC (London), the Köln Westdeutscher Rundfunk (Germany), NOS National Radio (The Netherlands), Zurich Radio (Switzerland), the Television Broadcasting System (Japan) as well as for the United States State Department for broadcast on its 'Voice of America' program. The CSUN Wind Ensemble's recording with the Mirecourt Trio in 1982 was named the 'Record of the Year' by The Village Voice. Composers who have guest conducted Whitwell's ensembles include Aaron Copland, Ernest Krenek, Alan Hovhaness, Morton Gould, Karel Husa, Frank Erickson and Vaclav Nelhybel.

Dr. Whitwell has been a guest professor in 100 different universities and conservatories throughout the United States and in 23 foreign countries (most recently in China, in an elite school housed in the Forbidden City). Guest conducting experiences have included the Philadelphia Orchestra, Seattle Symphony Orchestra, the Czech Radio Orchestras of Brno and Bratislava, The National Youth Orchestra of Israel, as well as resident wind ensembles in Russia, Israel, Austria, Switzerland, Germany, England, Wales, The Netherlands, Portugal, Peru, Korea, Japan, Taiwan, Canada and the United States.

He is a past president of the College Band Directors National Association, a member of the Præsidium of the International Society for the Promotion of Band Music, and was a member of the founding board of directors of the World Association for Symphonic Bands and Ensembles (WASBE). In 1964 he was made an honorary life member of Kappa Kappa Psi, a national professional music fraternity. In September, 2001, he was a delegate to the UNESCO Conference on Global Music in Tokyo. He has been knighted by sovereign organizations in France, Portugal and Scotland and has been awarded the gold medal of Kerkrade, The Netherlands, and the silver medal of Wangen, Germany, the highest honor given wind conductors in the United States, the medal of the Academy of Wind and Percussion Arts (National Band Association) and the highest honor given wind conductors in Austria, the gold medal of the Austrian Band Association. He is a member of the Hall of Fame of the California Music Educators Association.

Dr. Whitwell's publications include more than 127 articles on wind literature including publications in Music and Letters (London), the London Musical Times, the Mozart-Jahrbuch (Salzburg), and 39 books, among which is his 13-volume History and Literature of the Wind Band Ensemble and an 8-volume series on Aesthetics in Music. In addition to numerous modern editions of early wind band music his original compositions include 5 symphonies.

David Whitwell was named as one of six men who have determined the course of American bands during the second half of the 20th century, in the definitive history, The Twentieth Century American Wind Band (Meredith Music).

A doctoral dissertation by German Gonzales (2007, Arizona State University) is dedicated to the life and conducting career of David Whitwell through the year 1977. David Whitwell is one of nine men described by Paula A. Crider in The Conductor's Legacy (Chicago: GIA, 2010) as 'the legendary conductors' of the 20th century.

'I can't imagine the 2nd half of the 20th century — without David Whitwell and what he has given to all of the rest of us.'
                                    Frederick Fennell (1993)

www.ingramcontent.com/pod-product-compliance
Lightning Source LLC
Chambersburg PA
CBHW081154090426
42736CB00017B/3312